GULF SECURITY INTO THE 1980s

HOOVER INTERNATIONAL STUDIES
Peter Duignan, general editor

Publications in the Hoover International Studies series of the Hoover Institution on War, Revolution and Peace are concerned with U.S. involvement in world and regional politics. These studies are intended to represent a contribution to the discussion and debate of major questions of international affairs.

GULF SECURITY INTO THE 1980s

Perceptual and Strategic Dimensions

Edited by
Robert G. Darius
John W. Amos, II
Ralph H. Magnus

HOOVER INSTITUTION PRESS
Stanford University | Stanford, California

Hoover Press Publication 291

Copyright 1984 by the Board of Trustees of the
    Leland Stanford Junior University

All rights reserved. No part of this publication may be reproduced, stored in a retrieval system, or transmitted in any form or by any means, electronic, mechanical, photocopying, recording, or otherwise, without written permission of the publisher.

First printing, 1984
Manufactured in the United States of America
88 87 86 85 84   9 8 7 6 5 4 3 2 1

Library of Congress Cataloging in Publication Data
Main entry under title:
Gulf security into the 1980s.

    Includes bibliographical references and index.
    1. Persian Gulf Region—Politics and government—Addresses, essays, lectures.   I. Darius, Robert G.   II. Amos, John W., 1936–   .   III. Magnus, Ralph H.
DS326.G85   1984   953'.053   84-4577
ISBN 0-8179-7911-5
ISBN 0-8179-7912-3 (pbk.)

Contents

Editor's Foreword

The Persian Gulf region is volatile and unstable not only for the states within the region and for states surrounding the Gulf but also for states farther afield that depend on its oil. The Soviet presence in Afghanistan threatens and destabilizes both the Gulf states and Pakistan and India. The Carter Doctrine (offering to defend the area against Soviet attack), the development of the Rapid Deployment Force (RDF), and the West's need for oil require continued U.S. involvement in the politics of the region. The main immediate threat to the leaders of the Gulf states comes from Iran and Iraq, especially from Khomeini and his efforts to overthrow the leaders of the local states. But internal threats also come from the large number of immigrant workers in these states and from the Palestine Liberation Organization allied with Khomeini. U.S. efforts to make the Arabs aware of the Soviet menace have been unsuccessful to date. For Gulf leaders the Arab-Israeli dispute and the Iran-Iraq war appear more threatening to peace than Soviet troops in Kabul.

Both Iran and Iraq want to become the policemen of the Persian Gulf, much as the Shah was. Khomeini wants even more; he wants to export his Shi'ite religious revolution to all the surrounding states.

As the essays in this volume show, the Gulf states and Saudi Arabia formed the Gulf Cooperation Council (GCC) in 1981 to assure their own internal security and to avoid dependence on any external powers. While the Saudis and others approve in principle of the United States' RDF, they do not want its bases in the Gulf area. Some Arab leaders fear the intentions of the RDF in this oil-rich area—they believe the United States would use it to intimidate the locals or to seize their oil, not to fight the Soviets or so-called liberation movements. Even among the conservative pro-Western Arab leaders, the United States has problems.

The United States and its major allies will continue to be dependent on oil from the Gulf region for some time. There are no alternative sources of energy in the short run that can end that dependency. Since oil is vital to the industrialized states of the West and the Soviet bloc, the Persian Gulf area will remain a potential source of conflict between the superpowers.

The papers in this volume discuss clearly and forcefully these problems. Especially important to U.S. interests, the authors show, are the linkages between Gulf security and the Soviet presence in Afghanistan, Khomeini's foreign policy, the role of the Gulf war in Middle East politics, and the functions of the GCC. They also discuss U.S. policy and Gulf security. We are indebted to the contributors in this volume and to its editors for their cogent policy analyses.

Peter Duignan

Coordinator, International Studies
Hoover Institution

Foreword

The Persian Gulf is an old contest area among the major powers. Through the centuries the actors have changed. At one time or another, the Portuguese, the Dutch, the Iranians, the Arabs, the Turks, and the British appeared on the scene. Similarly, the focus of interest changed. Initially, trade and imperial communications provided the main motive force of great powers' policies. Later, the strategic location of the Gulf—because of its proximity to India— was a determining factor. And, in more recent times, oil tended to overshadow other considerations in shaping the Gulf's role in world affairs.

By the middle of the nineteenth century, Great Britain was fairly well entrenched in the Gulf. In erecting a chain of protectorates on the southern, Arabian side of the Gulf, Britain ensured its commercial and political supremacy, backed by the Royal Navy. At the turn of the century, Britain's predominant position was challenged by imperial Germany, whose Berlin-Baghdad railroad project signified a desire for expansion toward the Gulf. Almost simultaneously, czarist Russian ships began plying the Gulf waters with increasing frequency, leading to a possible establishment of Russian trading and naval outposts. Foreign Secretary Lord Lansdowne's declaration of 1903 represented Britain's reaction to these looming threats. Lansdowne warned the would-be intruders that any penetration into the Gulf would be resisted with all means at Britain's disposal, including the use of force.

Russia's revolution of 1917 and Germany's defeat at the end of World War I removed these actual or potential rivals from the scene for the next half of the century, permitting Britain to exercise uncontested supremacy in the Gulf.

However, during the 1950s two new challenges arose. On the one hand, U.S. private enterprise began to play a steadily growing role in the oil affairs of the region. On the other, the emergence of militant Arab nationalism stimulated by Gamal Abdul Nasser's leadership posed a threat to the intricate mechanism of British-tribal-dynastic controls over the sheikhdoms of the Gulf and the periphery of the Arabian Peninsula. Thus the American commercial and Arab nationalist challenges contributed in the 1960s to the gradual erosion of the British position. Furthermore, the "will to empire" was waning in Britain, whose Labour governments, in and out of power, were preoccupied more with social security at home than with imperial ventures abroad.

There was a paradox in this situation. Because of Europe's growing dependence on imported oil, the strategic importance of the Gulf was increasing and yet Britain, which could act as a de facto trustee for the West's interests in the Gulf, was relinquishing her political and military dominance of the region. The process began with the independence granted to Kuwait in 1961 and by 1971 Britain put an end to her protectorate over the remaining Gulf principalities. Bahrain, Qatar, and the United Arab Emirates emerged as small but sovereign entities, while Oman—already formally sovereign—reasserted its independence.

Britain's departure created a politico-military vacuum in the region. Its rich oilfields fell under the rule and ownership of a group of mini-states whose capacity to protect them was drastically diminished just when Soviet interest in the Gulf and the whole Arab world was intensifying. This posed a serious problem to the United States: how to safeguard the region without appearing imperialistic. Moreover, new and disquieting phenomena began aggravating the situation: the Iranian revolution of 1979—with its connotation of expanding religious fundamentalism inimical to the established dynastic orders in the Arabian Peninsula; the Soviet occupation of Afghanistan; and the war between Iraq and Iran, begun in 1980, with the threat of spillover into the Gulf and the Arabian Peninsula. However reluctant to extend its military commitments following the trauma of the Vietnam war, the United States found it necessary to define more precisely its posture toward the Gulf and, through the Carter Doctrine of January 1980, to warn the would-be aggressors and infiltrators that it would resist an assault on the Gulf with the use of military force if necessary. Simultaneously, the formation of a Rapid Deployment Force was announced as a concrete step to implement the new military commitment.

This evolution of the international status of the Gulf found its reflection in the political literature. Initially, most of the writing was by the British, whose works on the Gulf combined history with an explanation, often with moral justification, of Britain's imperial mission. Typical of this attitude was the passage in Sir Arnold T. Wilson's classical work *The Persian Gulf*: "We have maintained order and thereby promoted trade; we have raised the standard of living and thereby encouraged the spread of education: we have thus fostered the growth of individual freedom and of aspirations to succeed in life. . .It is one of the wonders of history that, from this little island, men have gone out not merely to form a number of great, free nations, and to create a dependent empire, but to exercise in many regions —of which the Persian Gulf is only one—a moral influence, often without material backing, which has brought peace to waters which for a thousand years knew no security" (pp. 272–73). And, to stress the solidity and permanence of the British position in the region, Wilson opens his concluding chapter with a statement by the under secretary for foreign affairs in the House of Lords in 1924: "Our position in the Persian Gulf. . .is at the present time absolutely untouched and unassailable (p. 254)." The Gulf's importance as the most abundant center of oil was treated in the well-known work of another imperial-minded Briton, Sir Olaf Caroe, *Wells of Power: The Oilfields of South-Western Asia*, while an American scholar, Briton Busch, produced a richly documented historical study, *Britain and the Persian Gulf, 1894–1914*, which stressed the continuity and intensity of British involvement in Gulf politics and strategy.

Britain's impending, and then actual, withdrawal from the Gulf generated a number of studies, this time produced mostly but not exclusively in the United States. Their objective was, first, to explore the strategic importance of the Gulf and, second, to discuss the means whereby the region might be protected most effectively from encroachments hostile to the Free World, in general, and the United States, in particular. Various institutes and research organizations, such as the Georgetown Center for Strategic and International Studies, the Foreign Policy Association, the American Enterprise Institute, the International Institute for Strategic Studies, and the Hoover Institution, began publishing policy-oriented monographs.

Iran's aspiration to replace Britain's influence in the Gulf with its own stimulated two noteworthy studies in English: Rouhollah Ramazani's *The Persian Gulf: Iran's Role* and Abbas Amirie's (ed.) *The Persian Gulf and Indian Ocean in International Politics*. Furthermore, growing realization of the region's crucial role in world politics provided some longer and more detailed studies, such as John Duke Anthony's *Arab States of the Lower Gulf* and *The Persian Gulf States*, edited by Alvin J. Cottrell.

Defense and stability of the Gulf provide two leading themes of the present volume. The essays cover comprehensively the key aspects of Gulf security. As Robert Darius points out in his introductory chapter, security in the region is a multidimensional phenomenon. It has its local, regional, and international aspects. One might add that the Gulf may be considered in its narrower (ministates) or broader definition. If the latter approach is taken, then not only the attitudes of the Big Three—Iran, Iraq, and Saudi Arabia—must be considered but even those of the states not directly adjacent, such as South Yemen and Afghanistan. This explains why, in his pioneering essay, Ralph Magnus discusses the link between the Soviet occupation of Afghanistan and Gulf problems. Similarly, Gulf security cannot be treated in isolation from the Iraq-Iran war, whose "spillover effects," as analyzed by John Amos, may have profound bearing on the choice between the status quo and revolutionary change in the Gulf area. Even without that war, Khomeini's Iranian revolution of 1979 in itself was bound to produce mixed religious-political repercussions in the area—the subject of a separate chapter by Darius. Increased U.S. involvement in Gulf affairs is explored in an essay by Charles MacDonald. Last but not least, defense and stability of the Gulf have increasingly stimulated the Gulf states to explore ways of collective action. A study of the Gulf Cooperation Council by John Duke Anthony thus adds a new dimension to the problem of Gulf security.

The timing of this volume should have some bearing on the relevance of its findings. The authors of the essays have had the advantage of writing after the occurrence of certain events such as the Iranian revolution, the Soviet invasion of Afghanistan, the proclamation of the Carter Doctrine, the outbreak of the war between Iraq and Iran, and the formation of the Gulf Cooperation Council. Hence, their analyses have moved from the realm of speculation about the potential dangers in the Gulf area to that of dealing with the actual, present challenges to the security of the Gulf. This multidimensionality of Gulf security will be amply demonstrated in these essays.

George Lenczowski

University of California at Berkeley

GULF SECURITY INTO THE 1980s

1 | Introduction: The Multiple Dimensions of Gulf Politics and Security

Robert G. Darius

Security in the Persian Gulf region in the early 1980s will depend on the interaction of a number of complex factors, all of which affect the area. The Iranian Revolution, the Iraq-Iran war, the Soviet invasion of Afghanistan, the Carter Doctrine, and the development of the Rapid Deployment Joint Task Force (RDJTF) exemplify the range of internal, regional, and extraregional elements that will influence Gulf security in the 1980s. The convoluted and fluid situation in the Gulf area defies simple solutions.

Perceptions of threats to security vary in the Gulf area. Arab leaders view the most pressing and immediate threat mainly in the framework of the spillover of the Arab-Israeli or Iraqi-Iranian disputes. Iran's leaders see the principal threat to Gulf security in terms of superpower intervention and emphasize what they see as corruption and lack of legitimacy in the conservative, pro-Western Gulf states as the key internal source of domestic instability. Iran's rhetoric against the conservative, centrist Arab states fuels instability in the Gulf region.

U.S. attempts to develop a strategic consensus centered on the primacy of the Soviet threat face opposition in most Gulf states, where threats from the ongoing Iranian Revolution, Israel, and the "encirclement" of the Arabian peninsula by Soviet proxies are considered more immediate. The abortive

The views, opinions, and/or findings contained in this report are those of the author and should not be construed as an official Department of the Army position, policy, or decision.

U.S.-Israeli strategic cooperation agreement has raised serious questions in the Gulf area over the sincerity of U.S. attempts to play an evenhanded role between Arabs and Israel. This questioning, in turn, has further undermined U.S. attempts to develop a strategic consensus on the Soviet threat. The Israeli bombing of the Iraqi nuclear reactor and Israel's invasion of Lebanon have intensified Arab concern over the validity of such a strategic consensus.

King Fahd of Saudi Arabia is dissatisfied with U.S. policy in the Middle East, as it concerns the Palestinians, because of its ramifications for security and stability in the Gulf region. According to Gulf leaders, the Arab-Israeli dispute will continue to provide the Soviets with opportunities to make inroads in the entire area. Moreover, the war between Iran and Iraq and the likelihood of ethnic separatist movements provide further opportunities for Soviet influence. Although a solution to the Palestinian problem will not solve the other problems of security and stability in the Gulf area, it will increase U.S. influence in the Arab world, will make a positive U.S. role in Gulf security more palatable and acceptable, and will remove the key source of tension between the United States and the Arab world. Sheikh Zaki Yamani, the Saudi oil minister, has stated that although his country perceives the Soviets as a threat, the Saudis believe the Israelis are a much greater threat. As long as such a view prevails, it would be difficult to expect Arab leaders to support the United States in a concerted effort to prevent the Soviets from gaining additional influence in the region at U.S. expense.

The Soviet invasion of Afghanistan, the lack of U.S. credibility, the Gulf war between Iran and Iraq, U.S. efforts to ensure Gulf security unilaterally through the use of the Rapid Deployment Joint Task Force (RDJTF), plus uncertainty among the Arabs as to U.S. intentions concerning use of the RDJTF and Khomeini's intentions to export revolution to the Gulf states, have all contributed to expand ties between Iraq, Saudi Arabia, and other conservative states in the area. The Iranian revolution and Khomeini's ideological stance alone, however, are not the only sources of tension and cohesion among the Arab states. The establishment of the Gulf Cooperation Council (GCC) suggests that the Gulf states can cooperate to assure their own internal security. Saudi Arabia, the most influential state on the Arabian peninsula, has usually taken the lead in attempting to create political arrangements to stabilize the Gulf area. The role of Saudi Arabia in the GCC is a graphic example of Saudi leadership to make a concerted effort to ensure that peace in the region is secured by the states of the area, rather than by extraregional powers. The GCC currently excludes both Iraq and Iran, probably because of the prevailing concern among the conservative states in the area over Iranian and Iraqi ambitions to dominate the region.

In this regard, the conservative states of the Arabian peninsula are as wary of Iraq as they are of Iran. Iraq, as an Arab state, could be accepted as a member of the GCC if it applied for membership and if the GCC members could be convinced that Iraqi ambitions to dominate the Gulf were no longer valid. But it is unlikely that Iran would even consider joining the GCC, an organization dominated by conservative Arab regimes. And as long as Iran, the most populous state of the region, continues to espouse an aggressive forward policy toward the Gulf, an acute sense of insecurity will continue in the area. The GCC manifests the eagerness of the moderate Arab states to maintain a distance from the United States and the Soviet Union and to resolve Gulf security problems by themselves, without relying on external powers.

During the first conference of the GCC defense ministers in Riyadh in early February 1982, Prince Sultan, Saudi Arabia's defense and aviation minister, stressed that security and stability in the Gulf area are the responsibility of the states in this region. "Regional and international situations," Sultan noted, "have made it necessary for the six GCC member-countries to pool their resources and potentials, in order to achieve the highest level of coordination and guarantee the security and stability of each member country 'in the face of growing foreign interference.'" Sheikh Zayed, president of the United Arab Emirates (UAE), expressed a similar viewpoint when he stated that Gulf security could only be achieved when "the countries of the Gulf are allowed to live peacefully . . . without interference from foreign powers, and without the great powers trying to determine the area's fate."

For their part, the Saudis have given the United States tacit approval of the RDJTF, but oppose U.S. bases in the Gulf area. Most conservative Gulf states also remain apprehensive about the intentions of the RDJTF in the region. The centrist Arabs prefer to remain pro-Western but at the same time to avoid any actions that would make them appear "puppets" of the United States. Additionally, they remain suspicious about whether the United States intends to use the RDJTF as an instrument to intimidate the oil producers of the region or as a means to take over the oil fields in the future, should a dire need arise. This apprehensiveness in the Gulf area about the real intentions of the RDJTF remains a key obstacle to its deployment to shore up U.S. friends. It is questionable whether friendly states would ask the United States to deploy the RDJTF to the area to support them in time of crisis, particularly as long as they could meet the threat.

In their paranoia, based on two centuries of foreign intervention in their country, Iran's leaders see Washington as the principal source of the Gulf war, the problems with the Kurds, and other major domestic upheavals in Iran. These perceptions strengthen their negative view of Washington and increase their criticism of pro-Western Gulf states, particularly Saudi Arabia. U.S. efforts to defend the Gulf, as evidenced by the development of the RDJTF, by the deployment and ultimate sale of Airborne Warning and Control Systems (AWACS) planes to Saudi Arabia, and by U.S. encouragement of the GCC, are viewed in negative terms. Washington is caught in a dilemma: if it gets closer to the Arabs to help defend them against the long-term Soviet threat and the short-term threat of the possible spillover of the Gulf war, Iran would be encouraged to move closer to Moscow, to balance what it sees as a superpower game that may have an unfavorable end for Tehran. If Washington fails to assist the Arabs to defend themselves, it will lose credibility in the Arab world as their superpower friend. Washington's role in this delicate situation has to be played in a low-key, calculated fashion.

Despite current projections indicating a decreasing dependence by major Western oil consumers on the Gulf's oil, U.S. security interests in the Gulf area will revolve primarily around the need to ensure access to oil, primarily for Western Europe and Japan. It is conceivable that Western dependence on Gulf oil will continue to decline throughout the 1980s, but as long as that trend has not been definitively established and as long as the Gulf area holds the free world's largest known oil resources, it would be premature to discount its importance to the West. As long as the region's oil is vital, the area will remain vital to the United States. Even without oil, the Persian Gulf area is critical to the East-West balance of powers. Therefore, both the United States and the USSR will continue to covet the Gulf region and will try to deny each other hegemony over it.

As Ralph Magnus points out in the first of the six chapters that follow linkages between security in the Gulf area and events in Afghanistan have long been and remain a factor in Gulf security. The recent events that culminated in the Soviet invasion of Afghanistan, according to Magnus, have served "as a powerful catalytic agent on the nascent movement of the Gulf states toward political/security cooperation." Magnus places the linkages between Afghanistan and the Gulf states in historical perspective, from the British colonial era prior to the end of World War II (the era of Anglo-American cooperation), through the period of Iranian hegemony in the 1970s, up to the time of the Soviet invasion of Afghanistan, the ouster of the Shah, and the subsequent Gulf war. Weaving the influences of these historical periods into the backdrop for security in the Gulf area, Magnus evaluates the perceptions of the Gulf states in light of their efforts to achieve some security through regional cooperation in order to exclude a military role for either of the superpowers in the area.

Robert G. Darius next analyzes the sources and consequences of Khomeini's foreign policy and places this policy in the context of larger issues involving the collision of nationalism and religion in the Middle East. Darius concludes that as long as the present regime in Iran remains committed to exporting its version of the Islamic revolution, Gulf states will face continued sectarian pressure.

In the fourth chapter, John W. Amos, II, discusses the Gulf war between Iran and Iraq in the broader configuration of the Middle East. Amos not only examines the sources of the Gulf war but also identifies the connections between the sources of the conflict between Iran and Iraq and other disputes in the Middle East in intercommunal and intercultural terms. The chapter's in-depth analysis of the linkages among conflicts in the Middle East includes an examination of the effects of the Gulf war on the shifting alliance patterns between Iraq and its supporters on one hand, and Iran and its supporters on the other. The Palestinian issue and sectarian differences between the traditional Shi'a and Sunni sects of Islam are added to the factors involved in the rapidly changing politics of the Middle East.

The relationship of the Gulf Cooperation Council (GCC) to Gulf security is next analyzed by John Duke Anthony in the context of the quest for intra-regional cooperation along a broad spectrum of matters, of which security is one. The GCC, which consists of Saudi Arabia, Kuwait, Bahrain, Qatar, the United Arab Emirates, and Oman has attracted considerable attention in the Gulf area and in the West since its establishment in January 1981. Anthony examines the GCC as the most recent manifestation of intraregional quests for cooperation; analyzes the origins of GCC, its significance, and its development; and offers an assessment of its prospects for the future in economic and social, as well as military and security, affairs.

Turning our attention to the West, Charles G. MacDonald in the sixth chapter analyzes U.S. policy and Gulf security on the basis of U.S. objectives to promote regional stability, to nurture friendly ties with the states in the Gulf area, and to ensure Western access to oil. Discussing U.S. reliance on Iran as the principal pillar in the twin-pillar policy based on the Nixon Doctrine, which proved to be involved with the Shah's ouster from power, MacDonald shows how the Nixon Doctrine was replaced by the Carter Doctrine, which relies on U.S. military power to protect vital interests in the Gulf area. As MacDonald points out, U.S. policy focuses on the possibility of Soviet threats by radical states in the region as well as on internal threats and terrorism. The methods used by the Reagan administration to attain U.S. policy aims rest on strengthening the RDJTF, providing security assistance to U.S. friends in the area, and securing facilities-usage agreements for the RDJTF. MacDonald concludes, however, that major problems face the United States in the Gulf area, including the movement toward nonalignment; the linkage of Gulf politics to the Arab-Israeli dispute; and the effects of massive amounts of security resistance on traditional societies in the Gulf area, as well as the effects of Libyan and Iranian efforts to export revolution to the region. MacDonald concludes that U.S. policy will be crucial to enhancing regional stability, if it is sufficiently flexible to meet the challenges and political dynamics of the Gulf area.

Taken together, these five analyses illustrate the complexities of Gulf politics. They also illustrate the difficulties facing U.S. (and other Western) policymakers in developing strategies designed to stabilize the Gulf area internally and defend it from external threats. As a problem for the foreseeable future, Gulf security will present policymakers with a continuing challenge.

2 | Afghanistan and Gulf Security: A Continuing Relationship

Ralph H. Magnus

The international politics of the Persian Gulf region and Afghanistan are intimately and inexorably linked; events in one have had an immediate impact on the other. This has been the case from the early nineteenth century, beginning with the close relationship of Great Britain and the two regions. It is all the more true of the most recent era, since the Soviet invasion of Afghanistan at the end of 1979.

There are a number of factors working to influence the political dynamics of each area. While not denying the multiplicity of causation, this study examines the linkages between the major political events in Afghanistan, particularly in the 1970s, and the larger structure of international relations in the Gulf and South Asia. During that decade, the dynamics of the Afghan situation may be traced to events in the regional environment; since then the reverse has been true. In the early 1980s, the situation in Afghanistan became an important factor in the movement of the Gulf states toward regional cooperation for their mutual security.

This trend has important consequences for the policies of both the regional states and the superpowers. The consolidation of the Soviet domination of Afghanistan, while not presenting insurmountable problems from the purely military standpoint, could create a climate in which the Gulf states, including

---

The views, opinions, and/or findings contained in this report are those of the author and should not be construed as an official Department of the Navy position, policy, or decision.

Iran, would move to adjust their security policies to the new situation of Soviet regional hegemony. The restoration of an independent and nonaligned Afghan government and the withdrawal of the Soviet occupying forces, while not causing an immediate relaxation of regional and Western-sponsored cooperative efforts, could slow the momentum of these efforts and ultimately cause them to atrophy in the manner of the former Central Treaty Organization (CENTO). The current situation of instability in Afghanistan—with the Soviet Union unable to consolidate the extension of its empire and the United States moving to counter further direct advances—acts as a continual reminder to the Gulf states of the need to consolidate and expand their own cooperative organs. It also serves to make the military and political presence of the United States in the region, if not overly popular, at least tacitly acceptable as a necessary counter to the demonstrable Soviet expansion.

British Imperial Hegemony

It was a fundamental premise of British policy that the defense of the Indian empire was impossible if it was limited to the defense of India's international boundaries. No major European power, be it France, Germany, or Russia, could be allowed to reach those borders. Britain had to expand the empire to a securer physical boundary, such as the Hindu Kush mountains of Afghanistan, or protect the actual border by a ring of buffer-states. As a result of the nineteenth-century wars in Afghanistan, the British concluded that the costs of maintaining a strategic frontier on the Hindu Kush would be excessive. The buffer-state solution was the rule, and expansion into Afghanistan was an aberration. With the British withdrawal from Afghanistan in 1881 following the Second Afghan War, this policy was formalized in agreements between Amir Abdur Rahman Khan and the government of the viceroy. By extension, Britain's initial interest in the Persian Gulf stemmed from the Gulf's position as a major route to the Ottoman and Persian dominions, which, along with Afghanistan, formed the belt of buffer-states for the Indian empire.

A gradual shift in emphasis appeared in the twentieth century. Due to the discovery of oil in the region in 1908, the Gulf became an important area in its own right, as well as a defensive buffer for India. The British could dispatch naval, air, and ground forces from the Indian subcontinent into the Gulf when needed in emergencies, while in normal times a few naval vessels were sufficient to secure Britain's political and economic interests.

Although British influence declined in Afghanistan and Iran following the 1914–1918 war and that of the Soviet Union increased correspondingly, the net effect on the security of the Gulf and the Indian empire was minimal. The strongly nationalistic governments of the region were anxious to maintain their independence from foreign powers. Nevertheless, Britain established new bases in Iraq by treaty with the Hashemite government. The new government in Russia, after a brief period of revolutionary adventurism, soon turned its attention to internal problems, including the task of re-establishing Russian power in the Caucasus and Central Asia. In 1937 the independent states of the region, Afghanistan, Iran, Iraq, and Turkey, came together in the Sa'dabad Pact to maintain this independence against both regional and more distant threats.

Anglo-American Security Cooperation, 1945–1968

The regional security situation altered profoundly after 1945. The most important change stemmed from the British withdrawal from India-Pakistan in 1947. This action, along with the grim postwar economic conditions in Britain itself, caused the British to inform their American ally that they no longer could be solely responsible for the security of the buffer-states against possible Soviet moves. Within the Gulf, however, the British concentrated their limited remaining resources on the immediate defense of the oil resources so vital to the West. Making this task much more difficult were increased nationalism, a more active Soviet opponent, and the loss of the strategic depth and reserves formerly provided by India. The new British policy involved a rough division of labor, with the United States assuming the responsibility for forward defense of the area against the USSR, while the British took care of the smaller states of the Gulf. The last chief commissioner of the Northwest Frontier Province of the Indian empire, Sir Olaf Caroe, promoted this new concept in articles, lectures, and a book, *The Wells of Power*, as well as in unofficial talks with U.S. leaders.[1] Caroe argued that the security of the Gulf was the key to the security of the entire Western world. It could be maintained only with the cooperation of the United States and Britain, along with that of the successor states of the Indian empire. Initially, Caroe hoped that India and Pakistan would join in this effort. When India refused to do so, he settled on Pakistan as the regional state most likely to aid in the defense of the Gulf.

The outbreak of the Korean War in June 1950 converted U.S. policymakers to Caroe's theories. U.S. policies designed to create a new defense structure had to await the solution of a number of pressing regional issues, however, such as the Iranian oil nationalization crisis of 1951–1954 and the future of the Suez bases, as well as the change of administrations in the United States.[2] President Eisenhower and Secretary of State John Foster Dulles worked for the creation of a Northern Tier alliance. U.S. policymakers viewed the coalition that emerged in the Baghdad Pact of 1955 with mixed emotions and saw the inclusion of Iraq as premature. The conflict between the Arab states and Israel began to be a distracting factor in developing a security structure in the Gulf; the Baghdad Pact excluded Israel from membership, and this proved to be a major reason why the United States found it impossible to adhere to it. In time, U.S. cooperation with the activities of the pact, especially after Iraq's withdrawal in 1959, constituted de facto membership.

The postwar period brought about a reassessment of the security situation by the regional states as well, and not the least affected was Afghanistan. Afghan leaders had come to make the best of their buffer-state position, which, if nothing else, had the advantage of familiarity. Few Afghans had expected that the British would carry out their pledges to withdraw from India. The new situation presented both opportunities and dangers. Afghanistan had never accepted the de facto border of the Durand Line as a de jure division. Indeed, during the course of World War II, they had discussed their territorial ambitions with the Germans, hoping that a British collapse might allow them to regain the lost Afghan empire stretching to the Indus River.[3] The ruling elite and royal family of Afghanistan were Pushtuns, as were the majority of the population of the Northwest Frontier Province. Balancing this opportunity to expand, however, was the loss of the British counterweight to the USSR.

Afghan policymakers resolved to pursue two aims simultaneously: they would replace British power with that of the United States, and they would press their Pushtun claims with the new government of Pakistan. They failed on both counts. The new Muslim state proved to be a more formidable opponent than they had bargained for. Nor would the United Nations get involved in rectifying the injustices of imperialist-imposed borders. For its part, the United States judged that the Afghan overtures were not worth the cost of Pakistani alienation. After a final attempt by the new and dynamic Afghan premier, Sardar Mohammed Da'ud Khan, to achieve an agreement with the United States, Afghan rulers turned to the Soviet Union for political backing of their claims to Pushtunistan, as well as for military and economic aid.

The shift in orientation marked a significant break with past practice; the Afghans had always preferred aid from more distant countries and feared too close relations with their powerful neighbors. This decision was justified in a Loya Jirgah (the great or general assembly of elected and appointed tribal, religious, and national leaders, convened periodically by the government to decide on major constitutional or foreign policy issues) as a necessity in light of Afghanistan's weakness and underdevelopment and the U.S. military alliance with Pakistan. Soviet premier Nicolai Bulganin and party chairman Nikita Khrushchev visited Kabul in December 1955; a series of economic and military aid agreements soon followed. The Afghans, however, were by no means willing to break their ties with the West; rather they sought to maintain and to increase the economic aid they were receiving from the United States and other Western nations.[4]

In the following decade, this tilt toward the USSR yielded mixed results for Afghanistan. The modernization of the military forces did enable the government to assert its authority more effectively in the provinces and thus permitted a more active policy of social and economic reform to be adopted.[5] The Pushtunistan policy, however, proved to be unproductive. Although Afghanistan grew stronger, Pakistan maintained its relative advantage by virtue of U.S. aid to the administration of President Mohammed Ayub Khan (himself a Pushtun). The dispute over Pushtunistan resulted in a closure of the Afghan-Pakistan border, physically isolating Afghanistan from the Western aid needed to balance the growing Soviet presence. Clearly, this was much further than even Sardar Da'ud Khan wished to go in his policy. Early in 1963, influenced by personal, familial, and internal political reasons, as well as by the foreign policy impasse created by the stalemated Pushtunistan issue, King Mohammed Zahir asked for his cousin's resignation.

With the help of Iran and the United States, the immediate problem of the border closure was resolved; the Pushtunistan issue remained dormant for the next decade. To be sure, political, economic, and military connections between Afghanistan and the Soviet Union remained close, but Afghanistan was now more truly nonaligned. Eastern and Western ties were carefully balanced, and aid flowed in from both sides.

The Gulf security situation at the time might best be termed an Anglo-American condominium. The United States supported the Baghdad Pact and its successor, CENTO. This role was formalized with the signing of bilateral security agreements in 1959 with Turkey, Iran, and Pakistan. The first article of these agreements, by reference to the Eisenhower Doctrine resolution of March 1957, made it clear that security cooperation "including the use of armed force" was to be directed against threats from "states controlled by international communism."[6] (In contrast, Britain's contribution to Gulf security was much broader; the first article of the Baghdad Pact stated that the members "will cooperate for their security and defence."[7]) Even more important, Britain's role stemmed from its treaty commitments to the smaller Arab states of the Arabian peninsula. In 1961 this commitment proved to be crucial in securing the independence of Kuwait.

Despite the withdrawal of Iraq from the Baghdad Pact in 1959, the loss of British bases there, and the growing dissatisfaction of the regional members with the lack of support from the United States and Britain in regional disputes, the essential security purposes of the alliance were achieved. Regional Cooperation for Development (RCD), founded in 1964, was an attempt on the part of the regional CENTO members to supplement their ties in the economic and cultural fields, as well as an assertion of their desire to develop a more independent international image. They hoped that in an era of international détente this image would prove to be attractive to other regional states, including Iraq and Afghanistan, and that something like the old Sa'dabad Pact might thus be revived.[8]

Direct U.S. involvement in Gulf security was symbolized by the continued presence of a small naval force based at the British facilities at Bahrain, as well as by closer involvement in the security of Saudi Arabia. Thus, in the early and mid-1960s, the United States made public commitments backed by military deployments in response to tensions stemming from the civil war in Yemen. Despite these commitments, both the United Arab Republic and Saudi Arabia accepted the United States as a mediator in their disputes arising out of the Yemen conflict.[9]

In the 1950s and 1960s, the security situation in the Gulf and Afghanistan remained essentially unchanged from that established at the end of World War II. The Anglo-American security guarantees and deployment of forces protected the Northern Tier states from direct Soviet threats and the Gulf states against regional and internal challenges. Pakistan provided depth to the alliance, as Caroe had envisioned. Afghanistan had been restored to its traditional buffer-state role—presumably with the consent of the Soviet Union. This condition of relative peace and security was, however, not to endure.

A Struggle for Hegemony: Regional and International

The era of rapid and increasingly drastic change began with the dramatic announcement of the British government in 1968 that it was planning to give up its security commitments "east of Suez." A transition period until the end of 1971 would allow new arrangements to be made. In contrast to the situation in 1947, the United States did not step into the breach. U.S. commitments to defend the Gulf against Soviet aggression would continue, but the Gulf states would have to provide for their own internal security. The United States would encourage this and provide arms, but would not make additional commitments. A cautious policy of limiting direct commitments of U.S. military support was an outgrowth of the lessons of Vietnam. This evolving policy, the Nixon Doctrine, relied on the states of the region, especially Iran, to guarantee the security of the region while the United States provided an overall guarantee against the possibility of direct Soviet aggression.

The newly emerging international system in the region was to be shaped by two distinct but interrelated processes, external and internal.

Internally, the Gulf states moved to gain control over their own oil resources. These resources would enable them to finance both internal development and military security. Although some new disputes did arise in the arena of petroleum politics, the overall effect of oil was to enhance regional cooperation. Each of the major states had more than enough oil, and world demand was rising rapidly. Thus, even at the peak of hostile relations between Iran and Iraq in 1971, Iraq could accept the Shah as a negotiator on behalf of the Gulf states in their talks with the international oil companies.[10] In 1975 the threat of full-scale war to their respective oil economies and the need for unity among the Organization of Petroleum Exporting Countries (OPEC) member-states, brought the Shah and Iraqi president Saddam Hussein to a compromise in the Algiers agreement. The development of this relationship created a climate of cautious détente that endured up to the fall of the Pahlavi dynasty in 1979.

At the same time, the greater financial resources and the greater scope for local action caused by the British withdrawal did lead to the assertion of a number of competing goals and policies, as some states moved to claim the fallen mantle of regional hegemony. Iran, supported by the United States, was the most successful in its ambitions. It occupied the Gulf islands of Greater and Lesser Tunbs and Abu Musa, intervened militarily against local insurrections in Pakistani Baluchistan and Oman, and engaged in an active military and diplomatic policy in the region. Iraq entered the contest for hegemony as well, seeking influence with the smaller Gulf states and even attempting to undermine the security of Pakistan. Following the Algiers agreement of 1975, however, Iraq adopted a moderate stance within the Gulf and the subcontinent, while attempting to assert a wider leadership role in the Arab world as a whole.

The net result of these crosscutting patterns of conflict and cooperation, fueled by fabulous oil wealth, was a stalemate. The Gulf states did not actively threaten each other's security and could even cooperate in practical matters to a significant degree. At the same time, underlying distrust made it impossible to construct a formal regional organization embracing all of the Gulf states.

The external factor in the new system was the conflict between the superpowers. Initially, this was muted. The United States continued its security guarantees to the Northern Tier, but for lesser problems, even those involving Soviet-aided subversion in Oman, it left the regional states to their own resources. Such was the spirit of détente that the United States and the Soviet Union held a series of talks on mutual force limitations in the Indian Ocean. As late as June 1979, after the fall of the Shah and the coup in Afghanistan, both the Soviets and the Americans endorsed the idea.[11]

Despite this endorsement, the Soviet Union actively worked to undermine the Western economic and military position in the region: through aid and diplomacy whenever possible or through subversion and military force when necessary.

Within two months of the announcement of the British intention to withdraw, the Soviets demonstrated their interest and intention to become a significant factor in a new Great Game for the high stakes in Southwest Asia.[12] A naval squadron from the Soviet Pacific fleet began a four-month cruise of the Persian Gulf and Indian Ocean, visiting India, Ceylon, Pakistan, Iraq, Iran, South Yemen, and Somalia.[13] By themselves, these deployments scarcely threatened the region or Western interests. They became a threat only when added to the inherent instability of the region, the accelerated changes brought about by the new oil wealth, and the lack of an effective counterforce. A broad and fertile field opened for Soviet activities designed to undermine the security of the region and the vital interests of the West.

The Position of Afghanistan in the 1970s

Afghanistan experienced four significant reorientations of its international position in the 1970s; three of these were the products of a violent change of regime. All, to a significant extent, involved the relationship of Afghanistan to the Soviet Union. In brief, the changes were

1. Sardar Da'ud Khan's coup of July 1973, which overthrew the monarchy and established a leftist-oriented republic;
2. The gradual but decided shift of President Da'ud's regime away from dependence on the USSR and toward accommodation with his regional neighbors, accompanied by the internal consolidation of his regime with the removal of his communist allies from positions of power;
3. The bloody communist-military coup of April 1978 establishing the Democratic Republic of Afghanistan;
4. The Soviet invasion of December 1979, resulting in the murder of Hafizullah Amin and the establishment in power of the Parcham faction of the communist party under Babrak Karmal.

Each of these events was intimately related to the wider struggle for regional hegemony characteristic of the post-1968 era, following Great Britain's announced intention to withdraw from its security commitments east of Suez. One point should be made clear at the outset: although the formal position of the royal government of Afghanistan was nonaligned and, if anything, closer to the USSR than to the West, in regional terms it favored the status quo. As long as Soviet aims in the region were limited, this was not a matter of great importance, even though this situation favored a pro-Western status quo. In fact, there was some compensation for the Soviets—they could point to Afghanistan as an example of their disinterested friendship and concern for a poor and underdeveloped neighbor, despite the differences in their forms of government. In the new situation, this was not enough.

Still, the Soviet relationship with the Afghan government was ambiguous, and there was some reason to believe that Afghanistan could prove useful to Soviet purposes. The extensive programs of military and economic aid, with the military side virtually a Soviet monopoly, allowed almost unlimited opportunities for the infiltration of Soviet nationals and Soviet-trained Afghan agents into all levels of the military and civil bureaucracies. Afghan government leaders were aware of these dangers, but felt that they could be countered by their own security services and by the strong nationalism of most Afghans. They felt that the main danger was the spread of communist propaganda to the general population; hence they turned to the West in general and to the United States in particular for educational aid, materials, and teacher training. One of the products of this program was Hafizullah Amin, the recipient of a master's degree in education from Columbia University.

The liberalization of the political system as a result of the constitution of 1964 (itself largely a result of the influence of Western democratic ideas) worked in favor of the USSR.[14] Some of the most active and well-organized of the political factions functioning as de facto political parties were Marxist groups. These were openly favorable to Soviet interests. Perhaps the most promising factor from the Soviet point of view was the possible revival of the Pushtunistan issue. Although Kabul had not pressed the issue since 1964, Afghan leaders were convinced of the justice of their claims. Their disinclination to advance this cause might well have been due to natural caution, given the remote chance of success and the fate of former prime minister Sardar Da'ud Khan's policies. Had conditions been more favorable, they might well have revived the Pushtunistan issue.

Sardar Da'ud's Coup, July 1973

The overthrow of the Afghan monarchy was the product of a number of diverse forces. Some of these were purely internal and, indeed, had little to do with Soviet policy and much to do with relationships within the Afghan royal family. Others were external: the regional and international system and the role of the Soviet Union in particular. The new importance of Afghanistan stemmed from the effects of the Indo-Pakistani War of 1971 and the emergence of Bangladesh. As the long-smoldering conflict between East and West Pakistan burst into open civil war in the spring of 1971, the Soviet Union concluded a "treaty of peace, friendship, and cooperation" with India. India invoked the military clause of the treaty on the eve of its offensive in East Pakistan.[15] Despite the tilt of the United States toward Pakistan, backed by the deployment of a carrier battle group in the Indian Ocean, Pakistan lay dismembered and prostrate in early 1972.

What was the reaction of Afghanistan to these dramatic events? Did it rush to take advantage of the golden opportunity to assert the right of Pushtunistan to follow the example of Bangladesh? Not only did the Afghan government do nothing of the kind, but it supplied aid to Pakistan by providing a refuge for Pakistani civil aircraft and by facilitating the transit of military supplies from Iran and Saudi Arabia.[16]

For its part, Iran moved swiftly to support the new regime of Zulfikar Ali Bhutto. It warned India against further actions and provided direct military aid to counter Baluch insurgency in western Pakistan, which threatened the security of the neighboring Iranian province of Baluchistan and Sistan. Iran and Afghanistan resolved the major source of controversy in their bilateral relations: the dispute over the distribution of the waters of the Helmand River. The treaty signed in Kabul in March 1973 had wider implications for the region, as R. K. Ramazani has noted:

> After the British withdrawal from the Gulf and the Indo-Pakistani War in 1971, the settlement of the age-old dispute with Afghanistan seemed all the more important. Iran wished to concentrate attention on difficulties in the Gulf area and to be able to mediate, as the Shah had done in 1962, the differences between Afghanistan and Pakistan over the problem of Pushtunistan. . . The Iraqi treaty with the Soviet Union signed April 9, 1972, further intensified Iran's determination to remove the ancient Helmand River problem from its relations with Afghanistan.[17]

The setback for Soviet policy was evident in the spring of 1973. Despite two decades of penetration and cultivation, Afghanistan had sided with two of the major opponents of Soviet advances in the Persian Gulf and Indian Ocean region: Pakistan and Iran. This orientation of Afghanistan's foreign policy was no accident. In late 1972, King Mohammed Zahir had appointed an able and popular prime minister, Mohammed Musa Shafiq, and given him royal backing to bring order to the chaotic domestic political situation. Shafiq made it clear that he would override the obstructionist Wolesi Jirgah (the lower house of parliament) in both domestic and foreign policy, as he pushed through long-stalled legislation and concluded the Helmand Treaty. Afghan Marxist factions had vigorously opposed a number of these measures, including the Helmand Treaty and a foreign investments law. Elections were scheduled for the fall of the year, the third general election to be held under the 1964 constitution. It was possible that a strong pro-monarchist party under Shafiq's leadership would be able to stabilize the constitutional system and lead Afghanistan into a new era of regional cooperation. The coup of July 1973 prevented this.

The coup was carried out by a coalition of supporters of Sardar Da'ud Khan and the Marxists. A number of officers who became prominent at this time served in later communist governments, including Aslam Watanjar and Abdul

Qader (the latter was appointed acting minister of defense of the Karmal regime.)[18] The one member of the Shafiq cabinet to remain in office after the coup was the minister of the interior, Nematullah Pazhwak. In 1980 it was admitted in the *Kabul New Times* that he was a longtime member of Parcham, the communist faction headed by Babrak Karmal.[19]

The coming to power of Sardar Da'ud Khan, with the aid and key support of the local Communists, was too favorable a development for the Soviet Union to have been mere coincidence. Although by no means a Soviet puppet, Da'ud Khan was the Afghan leader who had opened the country to the Soviets in the 1950s and, even more important, was known to be strongly committed to the Pushtunistan issue. Indeed, it was largely his stubborn support for confrontation with Pakistan over this issue that had resulted in his forced resignation in early 1963. As Louis Dupree has noted, "Ironically, it was the 'Pushtunistan' issue mainly responsible for the resignation of Daoud Khan in 1963 that played a major part in his return to power in 1973."[20]

Given the openly acknowledged close ties of the Parcham leaders, particularly Babrak Karmal, with the Soviet embassy and the key position of Soviet advisers in the Afghan military, it is inconceivable that the Soviet Union had no warning of the carefully prepared and long-discussed plot. Former King Mohammed Zahir believes that Parcham planned the coup and his cousin joined it at a later stage in order to prevent the establishment of an even more radical regime.[21]

Almost inevitably, Da'ud Khan would have had to vindicate himself by adopting a regional policy challenging the increasingly unfavorable, from the Soviet point of view, status quo. The benefits to be gained by the direct participation of Communists in the Da'ud government were an additional bonus that might take a few years to yield dividends. But in the long run, the Soviets could use this key position to make certain that the regime that succeeded Da'ud Khan's would be even more pro-Soviet in both internal and international affairs. The coup foreclosed any possibility that the constitutional monarchy would become politically stable under the leadership of Shafiq.

Initially, it appeared that Soviet calculations were correct. President Da'ud delivered his first speech in Pushtu rather than in Dari, which he normally used in making speeches, and retained or appointed a number of prominent Communists to high military and civil office. The Helmand Treaty went unratified. Da'ud reopened the issue of Pushtunistan and supported the Baluch insurgency in Pakistan by allowing guerrillas to operate out of base camps in Afghanistan, which threatened not only Pakistan but Iran as well.[22] Some five months before the coup, in February 1973, Pakistani security forces had opened crates of "diplomatic mail" addressed to the Iraqi embassy in Islamabad and found submachine guns, magazines, ammunition, and radios, all of

Soviet manufacture and accompanied by Russian-language manuals, which Pakistan charged were destined for the Baluch insurgents.[23] It appeared that both Iraq, which had supported Iranian Baluch dissidents since 1968 and had concluded a treaty of friendship and cooperation with the Soviets in April 1972, and Afghanistan, through its support of Pakistani Baluch guerrillas, were working in tandem to undermine the authority of the Iranian and Pakistani governments in their respective Baluch provinces.

From 1973 to 1975, the foreign policy of the Republic of Afghanistan was strongly hostile to Pakistan. It openly proclaimed that the Pushtun and Baluch issues were not internal affairs of Pakistan. President Bhutto reciprocated by supporting anti-Da'ud Muslim fundamentalists under the leadership of Gulbeddin Hekmatyar in an armed insurrection centered in the Panjshir Valley north of Kabul in July 1975. The Afghans charged the Pakistanis with complicity in this rebellion.

The advancement of Soviet foreign policy objectives by the Da'ud government was well received and appreciated in Moscow. Thus, the Soviets were quiet when President Da'ud Khan moved to eliminate local Communists from positions of influence and to close their party newspapers. As so often in the past, the Soviet Union was remarkably indifferent to the fate of local Communists, provided its foreign policy objectives were advanced. In any case, the clandestine communist organization in the military and the cadre of Soviet advisers were still in place.

Da'ud Khan's Shift to the Right

It is impossible to set a single event or date as the key to the gradual shift of the Da'ud regime away from a pro-Soviet policy. More than anything, the new oil wealth of Iran and the other Gulf states after the price increases of 1973–74 made this shift possible. In 1974, the Shah of Iran pledged a billion dollars in aid for transportation and industrial projects, including a railroad from Kabul through Kandahar to the southern Iranian port of Bandar Abbas. Besides being the first railroad in Afghanistan, this would have provided an additional outlet to the sea, bypassing both Pakistan and the route through the Soviet Union to Europe. In 1976 Iran augmented this aid (which had by no means been spent, as the railroad project had been delayed) by a further pledge of $2 billion for Afghanistan's new Seven-Year Plan, scheduled to begin the following year. Thus, Iran intended to use the resouces supplied by its oil wealth from the Gulf to stabilize and ensure the security of the region through aid to a neighbor— aid that would wean that neighbor away from dependence on the Soviet Union. The delays in the actual outlay of funds (although possibly due to natural causes because of the scope of the plans involved and bureaucratic inefficiency) may have been due in part to the deliberate obstruction of mid-level communist sympathizers in the Afghan government.[24]

Iran was active on the diplomatic front as well, and here the Shah's activities bore more immediate fruit. In the summer of 1976, there was a friendly and successful exchange of visits between Presidents Da'ud and Bhutto. This exchange contrasted sharply with efforts, scarcely a year before, of each leader to undermine the government of the other. On 31 August 1976, the Afghan national holiday of Pushtunistan Day went virtually unnoticed in Kabul, where the central city square is named in its honor.[25]

In January 1977, Da'ud Khan moved to consolidate the domestic basis of his regime by convening a Loya Jirgah to approve the republican constitution. The new constitution provided for a single-party state and a strong presidential system. Naturally, Mohammed Da'ud Khan was elected the first president under the new constitution, but the appointment of a vice-president was delayed. Former prime minister Shafiq was released from detention and appointed an adviser to the president. The former strongman of the monarchy, General Sardar Abdul Wali, Da'ud's cousin and personal rival, was allowed to depart for exile in Rome. There was even speculation that Abdul Wali might be designated as Da'ud's successor.[26]

The Soviet leaders received first-hand confirmation of Da'ud's new orientation and confidence in his new policy during his last visit to the USSR, in April 1977. Here, the fatal flaw in the Afghan leader's character, an overbearing pride and self-confidence, caused him to challenge the Soviet leaders openly on their own ground. When Leonid Brezhnev suggested at a Kremlin meeting that Da'ud Khan dismiss the Western experts working in Afghanistan, Da'ud replied that Afghanistan was an independent country and that if he got rid of some foreign experts, all of them would go. On a stopover in Tashkent, he stalked out of an official reception in anger when his host's speech linked the future of Afghanistan to those of the Soviet Union's Central Asian republics. On the return flight to Kabul, he spoke openly of his determination to rid Afghanistan of excessive Soviet influence.[27] One of those present was Mohammed Khan Jalalar, the minister of commerce. Jalalar was one of two members of the Da'ud cabinet (the other being Faiz Mohammed, frontier and tribal affairs minister, who was assassinated by the mujahidin) to continue in high office under the communist regime and in 1983 was in his old job once again.

These developments came at a most unwelcome time for the USSR, and the subsequent Soviet policy reassessment must have been agonizing. The Pakistani elections of March 1977, instead of confirming the seeming stability of the Bhutto government, created a wave of protests similar to those that had signaled the downfall of Bhutto's original mentor, Ayub Khan. In July the military chief of staff, General Zia ul-Haq, stepped in. Now, just when favorable opportunities were emerging in Pakistan, Afghanistan was moving in the opposite direction. Afghanistan had tapped the oil wealth of the Persian

Gulf, and President Da'ud and his brother and close adviser, Mohammed Na'im Khan, asserted their nonaligned credentials by embarking on a series of state visits to Yugoslavia and the countries of the Middle East and South Asia. As a price for Arab and Iranian support, President Da'ud seemed willing to give up the ancient ambition of his family—the reunion of the former Afghan empire and the Pushtun nation.

The counteroffensive of the Shah appeared on the verge of success. Tehran had convinced both Iraq and Afghanistan of the wisdom of peaceful coexistence and the regional status quo. The rebellions in both Oman and Baluchistan had been crushed, at least for the time being. At the same time, however, the Soviet Union began to adopt a more adventuristic regional policy as it shifted its support from Somalia to the military junta ruling Ethiopia.

The Khalqi Coup, April 1978

In July 1977, after more than a decade of bitter organizational and personal rivalries, the Khalq and Parcham factions of the Communists reunited as the People's Democratic Party of Afghanistan (PDPA). The titular leader of the united party was Nur Mohammed Taraki. His principal deputy, Hafizullah Amin, was given special responsibility for maintaining and increasing the secret organization of the party's military wing. Amin was ordered to prepare detailed plans for a military coup that could be launched on a moment's notice should Da'ud Khan's security services move against the party's leadership.

It strains credulity to believe that these two factions could have reunited without the aid of the Soviet Union.[28] Amin's military contacts, and his contingency planning as well, would have been impossible without the knowledge of the Soviet military advisers.

In any event, given the history of the final two years of the Da'ud regime and the actual timing of the coup, the question of whether the Soviet Union gave the final orders for its execution becomes largely academic. President Da'ud Khan's fate had been sealed a year before in that fatal meeting with Brezhnev in the Kremlin, and it had been precarious ever since his reconciliation with Bhutto in 1976. The Soviets' instrument had been forged with over twenty years of military, economic, and political penetration of the country. The union of the party in July 1977 put this instrument into the ruthless and able hands of those who would wield it on 27 April 1978.

Circumstantial evidence points to the possibility that the actual timing of the coup may have been accidental, a desperate response to Da'ud's decision to move against the party's leaders. Yet the chain of events leading up to the decision to act began with the assassination of a PDPA leader, Mir Akbar Khyber—an assassination at the time blamed on the government's secret police (but more likely the work of Amin or the Soviets). The funeral of

Khyber became the occasion for a large protest demonstration against both Da'ud Khan and the United States. This demonstration convinced the authorities to move against the party. Those who deny a Soviet role in the April coup have never been able to explain why the government had to resort to assassination when it could have simply arrested its opponents, and why, if it had caused the assassination, it did not take the obvious step of preventing the demonstration at the funeral.

In the context of the regional security situation in the Gulf and South Asia, the timing of the coup was most convenient for Soviet interests. The visit of President Anwar Sadat to Israel in the fall of 1977 had stirred deep opposition in the Arab states and diverted attention from Soviet moves to the east. The disturbances that eventually became the Islamic revolution in Iran were beginning in Tabriz and Qom. While it is evident that the Soviets, no less than the Americans, did not expect the fall of the Pahlavis, clearly these internal troubles diverted the attention of the Shah from events in Afghanistan. In addition, the situation in Pakistan had gone from bad to worse, as General Zia ul-Haq's martial law regime had arrested Bhutto on charges of murder and canceled national elections.

The United States was forced to deal with the weakness of its Iranian and Pakistani allies, as well as with the anger of the Saudis at the conduct of Sadat. At the same time, the opportunities opened by Sadat's dramatic initiative seemed too good to pass up. Thus, the energies of the Carter administration in the Middle East focused on the possibility of achieving an Arab-Israeli peace. The energies of the administration on a world scale, however, still centered on détente with the Soviet Union and the negotiations leading up to the Strategic Arms Limitations Treaty (SALT) II. It was difficult to convince anyone in a policymaking position of the importance of events in Afghanistan (not an easy proposition at any time). Even if they were convinced, it was inconvenient to raise distracting issues in U.S.-Soviet relations.

In contrast to 1973, the seizure of power in Kabul was quite bloody, even if brief. The new regime moved with caution in making changes in Afghanistan's foreign policy. Indeed, judging by the text of the announcement from Kabul, one might have suspected that the murdered former president was still alive and in charge. But two areas soon emerged as qualitatively different. One was the special position of the USSR. At the Belgrade meeting of the nonaligned states in July 1978, Foreign Minister Hafizullah Amin cited Afghan-Soviet relations as the model for Afghanistan's relations with all other nations:

> We hope that the Democratic Republic of Afghanistan's friendly relations with her historical friends and neighbors Iran and China and all the friendly countries of the world will expand in a form similar to our relations with the USSR, which are based on cordial friendship, independence, territorial integrity and non-

interference in each other's affairs. The friendly relations which exist between the Democratic Republic of Afghanistan and the USSR are a clear example of friendship between neighborly countries.[29]

Practically as well, the regime moved toward closer ties with the USSR by signing a large number of separate aid and cooperation agreements. The Da'ud government had agreed to most of these in principle, but Da'ud's reservations about the extent of Soviet penetration had delayed their signing.

The other major change was the re-emergence of the Pushtun and Baluch issues. The new government in Kabul mentioned them as matters that could be settled in peaceful negotiations (Pakistan's position was that they were purely internal matters and not the subject for international attention, peaceful or otherwise). On 7 May 1979, Radio Afghanistan broadcast congratulatory messages from some previously unknown Baluch "overseas representatives" of "the oppressed masses of Baluchistan"[30] Two days later, President Taraki and Deputy Prime Minister Karmal met with octogenarian Pushtun leader Abdul Ghaffar Khan, who was joined by Ajamal Khattak, an exiled leader of the National Awami party of Pakistan.

To Pakistan, these were disturbing indications that the Kabul regime intended to reopen the entire border nationalities issue that had been settled in the Da'ud-Bhutto talks and whose settlement had been confirmed after Zia ul-Haq took power. The worst case for Pakistan would be an attempt by the Afghans to carry out their propaganda by attempting to undermine the security and territorial integrity of Pakistan. Immediately following the Afghan coup, General Zia ul-Haq met with the leaders of the Pakistan National Alliance, who had agitated against Bhutto. A number of these politicians denounced the events in Kabul, but the National Democratic party of Wali Khan, the son of Abdul Ghaffar Khan, did not join in these statements.

The Gulf states and the United States responded cautiously. Officially at least, the new regime's program was not especially different from traditional Afghan positions, and it remained to be seen what these policies would be when put into practice. There was some reason to hope that a combination of Afghan nationalism and the precarious nature of a leftist government in a strongly conservative Islamic country would moderate both the revolutionary programs and the too-open attachment to the interests of the USSR. Publicly, the PDPA denied that it was either communist or Marxist-Leninist. The United States, Iran, and the Gulf States announced their recognition of the Kabul regime and continued their economic aid programs, on the theory that if the Afghan government were treated as an independent nationalist-reformist regime, it might tend to behave as one. Zia ul-Haq later claimed that he had attempted to warn the United States of the dangers from Kabul, but that the Americans had been indifferent:

The overthrow of the Da'ud government in April 1978 was anything but a harmless affair. This was well thought through and happened upon the instigation of the Soviet Union. But the Soviets stated they had no intention of interfering in Afghanistan and the Americans were not prepared to follow our interpretation. They believed that we were painting things in the gloomiest colors just to get aid and support. In the end it turned out, however, that we were right. [31]

Under the influence of its own rhetorical excesses, the relative ease of its seizure of power, and its initial acceptance by a broad group of intellectuals and bureaucrats dissatisfied with the slow pace of Afghanistan's progress, the new regime felt itself strong enough to attempt a rapid transformation of society from top to bottom. The continually repeated refrain of the leaders, which seemed to sum up their Marxist orientation, was that 98 percent of the population was oppressed and therefore in favor of the government's reform programs. The necessary corollary was that the 2 percent who were not in favor could easily be coerced. [32]

The reality was almost exactly the opposite. The regime was much weaker than anyone, even its enemies, thought. Part of this weakness was self-imposed. The Parcham faction of the PDPA, urban-based, largely of higher social strata, and Dari-speaking, urged a cautious national front strategy and more gradual revolutionary change. The larger Khalq faction ousted its leaders from office and persecuted, exiled, arrested, and even tortured them. The Khalqis were largely Pushtun-speaking, less well placed in society, and with strong rural ties; many were newly educated youths who had just moved to the city.

One consequence of the strategy of rapid social transformation was the necessity of importing even larger numbers of Soviet advisers. Many of these advisers came from the Central Asian republics; these republics, in turn, provided the model for the new society. Naturally, this caused widespread alienation with the Afghan bureaucracy. As internecine feuds within the party resulted in purges and desertions, the lack of qualified personnel became acute. A further consequence was the need for force. The attempt to bypass the rural social structure of tribal khans, village elders, and religious figures alienated the countryside, and in Afghanistan, the countryside is a permanently armed camp in a continuous state of incipient revolt against outside authority. Localized rebellions immediately sprang up throughout the provinces.

Previous Afghan governments would have retreated in the face of such opposition. The Khalqis instead reacted with massive and rapid repression, the end result of which was to spread the rebellion in a vicious cycle of expanded and better organized revolts. [33] By the fall of 1979, the conscript army had melted away to half its former strength. This desertion rate placed a great burden on the Soviet advisers. As the countryside was lost, there was no way to enforce the conscription system to replenish the ranks. Thus, although the opposition was divided into numerous competing groups based on ethnic, religious, and tribal lines, it was collectively growing into a genuine threat to the regime.

At this time, however, the attention of the Gulf states, and of most of the world as well, was riveted on the dramatic developments in Iran. Although the Afghan resistance leaders received a number of statements of support as they toured the Gulf states and other Middle Eastern countries, there was precious little governmental aid forthcoming. A trickle of money and arms began to arrive from Gulf and regional states (Egypt, Saudi Arabia, and Pakistan), but little reached the fighters inside Afghanistan. Their struggle, no doubt, was a worthy and an Islamic cause, but the regional governments, with the possible exception of Pakistan, did not yet consider Soviet influence a direct threat. It was still a civil war, and the governments of Afghanistan had long received Soviet supplies, including military equipment and advisers.

Indeed, it seemed that the international indifference to events in Afghanistan was justified. The inept PDPA regime was fighting for its life at the same time it was tearing itself apart internally; it was in no condition to pose a threat to anyone by engaging in foreign adventures. This assessment was mistaken. The new regime and the degree of Soviet involvement in it were not merely quantitative changes. The large number of Soviet advisers in key positions, including the military and the security services, had opened an entirely new option for Soviet policymakers; namely, massive and direct intervention. The new friendship treaty in December 1978 provided the cover of international legality so highly valued by the Soviets when they are contemplating aggression.

There were a number of immediate factors in the Soviet decision to eliminate the Khalq regime. One of these was the failure of the Afghans to follow the orders of the Soviets to use their influence on the antiregime Pushtun and Baluch nationalists to form a united front with the Pakistan People's Party to oppose the martial law government.[34] Another factor was Amin's refusal to allow the Soviets to take over the Shindand airbase south of Herat—this at a time when the Soviets feared U.S. military action as a response to the taking of the hostages in Tehran.[35]

All of these contributed to the Soviet decision, but the underlying reasons were more fundamental. The most important was that Amin's own stupid and brutal policies had narrowed his base of support in the educated elite and the party and had simultaneously swollen the ranks of his opponents, thus making the defeat of the communist regime all but inevitable. In March 1979, following serious fighting in Herat in which a number of Soviet advisers and their families were massacred, Amin had been named prime minister. He soon overshadowed his nominal superior, the Great Leader and president of the Democratic Republic of Afghanistan, Nur Mohammad Taraki. Amin's core of supporters in the army, security services, and state bureaucracy became too entrenched to be removed by political pressure, even when the Soviets succeeded in enlisting Taraki to attempt the task. This had been attempted in September when the Soviets persuaded Taraki to turn against his former right-hand man, Hafizullah Amin. Although willing, Taraki was ineffectual, and he paid for his failure with his life. The Soviets were then driven to play their last card, the Parcham and a group of anti-Amin Khalqis. They were a minority of a minority, but at least they knew how to take orders. A more sophisticated national front policy theoretically could have attracted enough popular support to defuse the rebellion. It was a policy that might have had a chance of success a year before, but there was no hope of success when it had to be imposed by Soviet troops.

The Soviet Invasion and the Gulf States' Response

The situation in Afghanistan was altered for the regional states as a result of the Soviet invasion. No longer could it be called a civil war; it was now a clear case of foreign intervention against a hitherto independent and nonaligned Muslim state. By his death at the hands of the foreign invaders, Hafizullah Amin had become (for the international community, if not for those Afghans who had opposed him) something of a national hero.

Unlike the April 1978 coup, the invasion hardly could be overlooked. The muted response of the Gulf states in 1978 was not repeated in 1979. In this response, a number of common themes can be traced. The Islamic element is certainly one of the most prominent. The open challenge to religious feelings stemming from the sight of Soviet forces fighting against a Muslim people could not be ignored. Immediately following the invasion, the Islamic states took the very significant action, which they have since maintained despite strong Soviet pressures, of denying the legitimacy of the Karmal regime. Beginning with an extraordinary meeting of the foreign ministers of the Organization of the Islamic Conference (OIC) in Islamabad in January 1980, the Islamic states have condemned the Soviet occupation of Afghanistan as a violation of its independence and called for the immediate, total, and unconditional withdrawal of all Soviet troops. Significantly, *all* Gulf states, including the Soviets' ally Iraq, have supported these resolutions, which have been reaffirmed in later regular meetings of the OIC foreign ministers in Islamabad (1980), Mecca-Ta'if (1981), and Niamey (1982). In the eyes of the Islamic states, there is no civil war in Afghanistan, but rather a war of national liberation against the Soviet occupying force.

A second element in their response has been the overt strategic threat posed by the advance of Soviet forces to the southern and eastern borders of Afghanistan, into Baluchistan and to within a few hundred kilometers of the Strait of Hormuz. For the Gulf states, it is reasonable to expect that the Soviets plan further military advances, even if on a contingency basis or in response to extraordinary opportunities. This expectation does not depend on the assertion of any grand design on the part of the Soviet Union; it is enough that it has a grand opportunity.

Perhaps even more important than the religious or strategic elements have been the revelations of the Soviets' behavior since December 1979. The use of regular forces in combat beyond their national borders in the Middle East is a significant escalation of their risk-taking in the region, an escalation that the regional states cannot ignore. Paradoxically, the more one believes that the Soviet action in Afghanistan, at least in its original motivation, was to save a deteriorating situation rather than part of a strategic advance, the greater the importance of this conclusion. If the Soviet leaders were willing to use force just to preserve a strategic position for future use, how much more willing would they be to take such action for a prize as valuable as the Gulf itself?

The overthrow of the Amin regime posed special ideological problems for radical regimes formally aligned by treaty to the USSR. Here was an example of a friendly, pro-Soviet regime being overthrown by Soviet intervention and another party faction installed in its place. Officially, this came as the result of a vote within the leadership of the PDPA ordering Amin's ouster and calling for Soviet aid on the basis of the friendship treaty. It was later revealed that Amin had all along been a CIA agent! The implications of this scenario were not lost on the Ba'th regime of Iraq, also allied to the Soviet Union by a treaty of friendship since 1972. As the Ba'th party newspaper pointed out:

> There is speculation, and we hope that it will not prove true, that the Soviet Union is now seeking partners in a relationship to ensure ideological and political expansion in the region, a method it has found to be preferable to relations of superficial friendship with other parties. For these relations— though based on friendship, progressiveness and a frank, sincere hostility to imperialism—do not guarantee the denied expansion...It appears that the Soviets have become interested . . . not only in a party that is sincere in its respect for relations of friendship with the Soviet Union, but in alternative parties that are inclined toward the USSR's short and long term strategy, rather than towards its friendship alone.[36]

The reaction of the Gulf states to the invasion of Afghanistan cannot be considered in isolation from the U.S. response. This response came quickly and unexpectedly in the form of the Carter Doctrine announcing that the

Persian Gulf region was a "vital interest" of the United States. Any attempt of an outside power to gain control of that region would be repelled by all means necessary , "including military force."[37] The seriousness of this declaration, if not its precise meaning, was emphasized by the deployment of major naval units and by the establishment of and efforts to secure facilities for the use of the Rapid Deployment Joint Task Force (renamed the U.S. Central Command in January 1983).

The establishment in 1981 of the Gulf Cooperation Council (GCC) of Saudi Arabia, Kuwait, Bahrain, Qatar, Oman, and the United Arab Emirates (UAE), along with other regional security moves, including close security cooperation between Saudi Arabia and Pakistan, was closely related to the situation caused by the invasion of Afghanistan. The Soviets aroused and confirmed deeply held religious, military-strategic, psychological, and ideological fears of their ambitions in the region. The use of force provided a new element of urgency to deliberations that led to the formation of the GCC. On the other side of the equation, the unaccustomed vigor of the United States' response aroused both positive and negative emotions. Positively, renewed U.S. commitments backed by force deployments in all probability forestalled a very different response—one based on fear and directed toward making the best possible accommodation with the new regional hegemonic power, the Soviet Union.

The Gulf states have rejected Soviet proposals for an international conference to "neutralize" the Gulf, such as voiced by Brezhnev on his visit to India in December 1980. A major reason for this continuing rejection is that acceptance of such proposals implies a recognition of the legitimacy of the Soviet actions in Afghanistan. Abdallah Bishara, the secretary general of the GCC, explicitly made this linkage:

> The neutrality of the Gulf cannot be separated from the neutrality of the adjacent areas—the Arabian Sea, the Indian Ocean, and the Red Sea. It would be futile to neutralize the Gulf while the Soviet troops are in Afghanistan and Soviet naval forces cruise the Indian Ocean or the Arabian Sea or maintain facilities in various Red Sea and Arabian Sea ports. Had the Soviet Union's proposal covered the neutrality of the Indian Ocean, the Red Sea and the Arabian Sea as well as the neutrality of the Arabian Gulf, and had the proposal involved the withdrawal of Soviet troops from adjacent areas, including Afghanistan, then it would have been sound and attractive.[38]

On the other hand, doubts of the effectiveness and constancy of the new U.S. posture, as well as the continued Soviet presence in Afghanistan, make any openly pro-U.S. alliance unlikely. This is true even if one leaves aside for the moment the issue of Palestine. Thus, Bishara found himself strongly criticized in the Gulf press for suggesting in another interview that the interests of the Gulf states and the United States "coincidentally" converge, even though this is merely accidental "and is not the result of planning or a previous study."[39]

The middle course of closer economic, political, and security cooperation thus seems a safer and, given the range of dangers faced by the Gulf states, a reasonably effective response. This allows those states least confident of U.S. determination and intentions, such as Kuwait, as well as those feeling most exposed and endangered, such as Oman, to come together in a common organization for their mutual security. Thus, although the events in Afghanistan were not in themselves sufficient to move the Gulf states toward regional cooperation, they were in all probability a powerful catalyst in this movement.

Notes

1. Olaf K. Caroe, *The Wells of Power, the Oilfields of South-West Asia: A Regional and Global Study* (New York: Macmillan, 1951).

2. Personal interview with Ambassador Loy K. Henderson, January 1972.

3. Ludwig W. Adamec, *Afghanistan's Foreign Affairs to the Mid-Twentieth Century: Relations with the USSR, Germany and Britain* (Tucson: University of Arizona Press, 1974), p. 246.

4. A revealing study of this era is that given by Ambassador Leon B. Poullada, "Afghanistan and the United States: The Crucial Years," *Middle East Journal* 35 (1981): 178–90.

5. The best treatment of the Da'ud Khan prime ministership is Louis Dupree, *Afghanistan* (Princeton, N.J.: Princeton University Press, 1978), pp. 499–558. On a more theoretical plane is his article, "Democracy and the Military Base of Power," *Middle East Journal* 22 (1968): 29–44.

6. For the text of the Eisenhower Doctrine, see Ralph H. Magnus, ed., *Documents on the Middle East* (Washington, D.C.: American Enterprise Institute for Public Policy Research, 1969), pp. 93–94.

7. Ibid., p. 81.

8. Personal interview with Dr. Abbas Aram, former foreign minister of Iran, Tehran, February 1972. In March 1972, while conducting research at the Tehran headquarters of the RCD organization, I was asked to carry a personal message to the Afghan deputy foreign minister at my next stop, Kabul, to the effect that Iran and the other members of the RCD would welcome Afghanistan's membership. The answer I received from Dr. Abdul Ghaffar Rawan Farhadi was that Afghanistan could not consider joining this organization as long as CENTO existed.

9. John C. Badeau, *The American Approach to the Arab World* (New York: Harper & Row, 1968), pp. 123–51.

10. George Lenczowski, *Middle East Oil in a Revolutionary Age* (Washington, D.C.: American Enterprise Institute for Public Policy Research, 1976), pp. 8–9.

11. "United States–Soviet Union—Conclusion of SALT II Strategic Arms Limitation Treaty, etc.," *Keesing's Contemporary Archives* 26 (1980): 30124.

12. Popularized in Kipling's novel *Kim*, the Great Game was the nineteenth-century contest for political, economic, and military power and influence between the British and Russian empires, particularly in Central Asia; see Kerr Fraser-Tytler, *Afghanistan: A Study in Political Developments in Central and Southern Asia*, 3rd ed. (London: Oxford University Press, 1967).

13. Alvin J. Cottrell and Frank Bray, *Military Forces in the Persian Gulf* (Beverly Hills, Calif.: Sage Publications, 1977), p. 8.

14. For the politics of this period, see Ralph H. Magnus, "The Afghan Constitution of 1964: A Decade of Political Experimentation," in Louis Dupree and Linette Albert, eds., *Afghanistan in the 1970s*, Praeger Special Studies on International Development (New York: Praeger, 1974), pp. 50–75.

15. S. M. Burke, *Pakistan's Foreign Policy: An Historical Analysis* (London: Oxford University Press, 1973), p. 403.

16. Personal interview with a former high Afghan official.

17. Rouhollah K. Ramazani, *Iran's Foreign Policy, 1941–1973* (Charlottesville: University of Virginia Press, 1975), p. 433.

18. Anthony Arnold, *Afghanistan: The Soviet Invasion in Perspective* (Stanford: Hoover Institution Press, 1981), p. 57.

19. *Kabul New Times*, 8 May 1980.

20. Louis Dupree, *A New Decade of Daoud?* American Universities Field Staff Reports, South Asia Series 17 (Hanover, N.H., 1973), p. 5.

21. Ralph H. Magnus, "Muhammad Zahir Khan, Former King of Afghanistan," *Middle East Journal* 30 (1976): 79.

22. The Helmand Treaty was later endorsed by the Da'ud government; see Selig S. Harrison, *In Afghanistan's Shadow: Baluch Nationalism and Soviet Temptations* (New York and Washington, D.C.: Carnegie Endowment for International Peace, 1981), p. 39.

23. Alvin J. Cottrell and R. M. Burrell, *Iran, Afghanistan, Pakistan: Tensions and Dilemmas* (Beverly Hills, Calif.: Sage Publications, 1974), p. 8.

24. Personal interview with Faiz M. Khairzada, former deputy minister of information and culture in the Da'ud government, 1981.

25. Arnold, *Afghanistan*, p. 64.

26. Shafiq had been released from detention and General Abdul Wali had been cleared by a court-martial in October 1975.

27. The Kremlin incident is cited in Arnold, *Afghanistan*, p. 65. Faiz M. Khairzada confirmed that this was common knowledge among high government circles at the time and added the information on the incident at Tashkent in a personal interview, 1981.

28. Arnold, *Afghanistan,* p. 65.

29. "Foreign Minister Amin's Address, Belgrade Nonaligned Meeting," *Foreign Broadcast Information Service (FBIS), South Asia,* 29 July 1978, p. C-1.

30. *FBIS, Middle East and Africa,* 7 May 1978, p. C-4.

31. "W. German Interview of Zia ul-Haq on Mideast Situation," *ibid.,* 12 March 1980, p. S-11. This is a report of a West German broadcast of 10 March 1980.

32. Personal interview with Mir Mohammed Siddiq Farhang, Washington, D.C., August 1981. Farhang was a deputy minister of planning and a member of the Wolesi Jirgah under the monarchy. He served as an economic adviser to Babrak Karmal in 1980.

33. "The Resort to Arms Was the Final Mistake," *MERIP Reports,* no. 89 (September 1980): 20–24. This revealing interview with "an Afghan Marxist" is excerpted from *Pakistani Progressive,* March–April 1980.

34. Alexander Dastarac and M. Levant, "What Went Wrong in Afghanistan," *MERIP Reports,* no. 89 (September 1980): 9. It originally appeared in *Le Monde Diplomatique,* February 1980.

35. This report has been attributed to Amin's mistress.

36. "*Ath Thawra* Discusses USSR Intervention in Afghanistan," *FBIS, Middle East and Africa,* 6 June 1980, p. C-1.

37. Ralph H. Magnus, "The Carter Doctrine: New Directions on a Familiar Stage," *Journal of the American Institute for the Study of Middle Eastern Civilization* 1 (Summer 1980): 3–21.

38. "Bishara Interviewed on GCC Issues," *Near East/North Africa Report,* no. 2383, *Joint Publications Research Service,* 18 August 1981, p. 21. The original interview by Mona es-Said was published in *Monday Morning* (Beirut), 20–26 July 1981.

39. "Daily Quotes Bisharah Remarks on Gulf Problems," *FBIS, Middle East and Africa,* 20 January 1982, p. C-1.

3 | Khomeini's Policy Toward the Mideast

Robert G. Darius

The Background for Iran's Mideast Policy

Events in Iran since the outset of the Iranian Revolution of 1978–79 have increased the degree of interest in the West toward Iran and its institutions. These events have also intensified the level of stereotyping prevalent toward Iran in particular and Islam in general. Despite the increased interest, Iranian affairs still remain shrouded in mystery for most people in the West.

Since its inception, the Islamic Republic of Iran has been heavily influenced by the personal traits, likes, and dislikes of Ayatollah Rouhollah Khomeini. The central figure of the Iranian Revolution, the frail but implacable 83-year-old Khomeini remains "the sole source of political legitimacy. When he dies, many believe, Iran could fragment into a fractional battleground, perhaps a civil war."[1] There is no doubt that civil war is a real possibility and a worst-case scenario for Iran. But there are a host of other alternatives.

Today the wealthy, the educated, and much of the Western-oriented, upper middle class have fled Iran; some have joined the opposition, and most have become disenchanted with Khomeini's clergy-dominated Islamic Republic. The armed forces are stronger, but still remain indecisive and weak. The clergy still commands mass support among the poor, illiterate, religious

The views, opinions, and/or findings contained in this report are those of the author and should not be construed as an official Department of the Army position, policy, or decision.

masses who form the vast majority of the population. Shi'a religious institutions, which the former Shah ignored, penetrate into all levels of society and provide the Shi'a clerics, or mullahs, with an existing political and religious structure for continuing in power. Mullahcracy, along with upheavals, is probably the most likely case in Iran, at least for the foreseeable future. As James A. Bill has pointed out, "The central and pivotal role" of religious leaders in the Iranian Revolution "cannot be overemphasized." Indeed, as Bill describes, Shi'a religious leaders "directed and then took control of the revolution": "From their mosques, schools, cells (hojrehs), and holy shrines, the Shi'a clerics personally and effectively put together an opposition organization that stretched from one end of the country to the other. It was this organization that mobilized the population and that was ultimately responsible for the collapse and destruction of the Pahlavi regime."[2]

Is the demise of mullahcracy in sight, as many Iranians in exile claim? Probably this is nostalgic, wishful thinking. Throughout history, major revolutions with popular, mass participation have usually been followed by prolonged periods of upheaval, as the French and Russian revolutions so clearly illustrated. Historians will be in a better position to judge the outcome of the Iranian Revolution. At this stage, one can only conjecture as to its ultimate direction. It is evident even from this near vantage point, however, that the Iranian Revolution has occasioned a deep and profound internal socio-economic upheaval, with potential far-reaching implications for other states in the Gulf area and in the Middle East. As William B. Quandt has noted, this Revolution was "unquestionably the most disruptive upheaval in the Middle East in the last generation"; in contrast to the Iranian Revolution, the Egyptian-Israeli peace accord was "a welcome development" for the West.[3]

Ever since the departure of the Shah in mid-January 1979, Khomeini has remained the key source of power in Iran. The struggle between Mehdi Bazargan's "moderate" de jure government and the Komitehs (committees of revolutionary zealots) and the extremist mullahs that served as the de facto government, ended after the seizure of the U.S. Embassy and the detention of U.S. diplomatic personnel as hostages. This sad and bizarre event illustrated Khomeini's belief that Iran should be free from the "hands of foreigners" and that diplomatic immunity was synonymous with the "capitulations" of the pre-1928 era.

More important, the hostage crisis of 1979 served as a vehicle in the internal struggle between "moderates" and extremist fundamentalists. Toward the end of that year, economic problems, the dual-layered government, the process of drafting the Islamic constitution, and stirrings of ethnic unrest all indicated the tempo of revolutionary upheaval as well as rising political discontent in Iran. The de jure Bazargan government was only a facade, since real power lay in the hands of the clergy and their Komitehs. The seizure of the

U.S. Embassy and the taking of the hostages provided Khomeini with an opportunity not only to utilize anti-American feelings to mobilize the population, but also to neutralize the so-called Westernized liberals who were allegedly prepared "to compromise with imperialism."[4] Such was the fate of Bazargan's government.

The ongoing Gulf war has also worked to the advantage of the extremist Muslim fundamentalists by enabling them to divert public attention away from divisive domestic issues and toward national unity against Iraq as the enemy. As R. K. Ramazani has noted, "The interplay between domestic and foreign policy should be considered in regard to the foreign policy of all countries,"[5] and certainly Iranian conduct of the war well illustrates the complex relationship of internal and external events as they have affected Iran in recent times. In the case of Khomeini's regime, the linkage between domestic and external policies is particularly crucial.

Characteristics of Khomeini's Regime

The general disparity of wealth; the high level of corruption, brutality, death, and midnight visits by the secret police; and other characteristics carried over from the former regime are by far the most valid descriptions of the new regime. Violence, injustice, and suffocation of basic human rights today in Iran are unsurpassed, while a new "dynasty" rising from the bosom of the mullahs is trying to solidify its rule in that country. Is this regime really new, or is it merely a repetition of Iranian history, in which dynasties appear and disappear like sandstorms?

Underlying cleavages between urban and rural, wealth and poverty, Shi'a and Sunni, minorities and majority, left and right, conservative religious masses and the middle class, and the tribal elements remain the principal sources of upheaval in Iran. Moreover, historic vestiges of Kurdish, Baluch, Azerbaijani, and ethnic-Arab divisions and grievances have not and probably will not disappear from Iran's political scene in the 1980s. These traditional divisions could only be swept under by sheer force, if a strong central government that could pacify them were to emerge in Tehran.

Such a government is not in sight. Ethnic and tribal unrest will grow as long as the central government remains weak. The outlying provinces of Iran lack the national control through the rural police (the gendarmerie) that was effective under the Shah; Khomeini has been unable to reorganize the gendarmerie into an effective force and to create a strong central government. The Pasdaran—the young, fervent supporters of Khomeini that have taken over the role of the gendarmerie—have thus far failed to establish order in Iran.

Fear, frustration, and uncertainty have resulted in a massive exodus from Iran, with numbers estimated in excess of 200,000 people and with many more waiting to escape from Iran. The result has been a shortage of professionals to operate and manage the country. Without the return of a fair portion of these professionals, Iran will remain crippled.

Khomeini's regime has also led to the decimation and purge of the top military leaders who served the Shah and could have probably served Khomeini. The loss of these leaders has led to disintegration and demoralization in the higher echelons of the military. As a result of the Gulf war, however, Khomeini has begun to rejuvenate the armed forces.

Khomeini's "Islamic" economic system is a shambles. Unemployment, underemployment, inflation, insufficient goods and services, housing shortages, the collapse of the industrial sector, and drastic cuts in oil production all illustrate the failure of the economy. It is doubtful that Khomeini could remedy these problems in the foreseeable future.

In addition to the economic problems, Khomeini's regime faces severe political problems. For example, underground opponents of the Islamic Republic killed about a thousand leading clergymen in the year after the 53 U.S. hostages were released. The clergy's grim response was to execute at least 2,150 people in the same period. The swift death sentences were carried out primarily against the Mujahidin Khalq, one of the principal organized opponents of the Islamic Republic, but others were executed who allegedly or actually violated Islamic tenents, including adulterers and drug dealers,[6] and also members of the Bahai sect.

The Pasdaran (revolutionary guards) fought the Iraqis, the Kurdish rebels, various bands of Baluch, and their own personal enemies, as well as the supposedly "pro-American and counter-revolutionary minigroups."[7] For their part, Kurdish rebels, monarchists, army deserters, and some members of the Mujahidin Khalq joined forces in the Kurdish areas against Khomeini.[8] Terrorist attacks against mullahs and their representatives and supporters continue by Marxists, supporters of the *ancien regime*, and ideological or ethnic dissidents. The immediate objective of the opposition is to seek revenge. For example, according to the clandestine Free Voice of Iran Radio, the opposition group that calls itself the Revenge Committee claimed credit for the attack on Mohammed Khamene'i, Majlis deputy and brother of President Seyyed Ali Khamene'i on 10 January 1982.[9] During the 1980s, the blood feud will continue, particularly among the large, extended families in Iran, as it still does in Lebanon.

In foreign affairs, the "'Great Satan' theory helps the clergy escape from the realities of domestic disunity, of ideological divisions, and of basic structural flaws in the Iranian society."[10] The exploitation and creation of anti-American sentiment, accompanied by the view that an invisible hand moves behind the scenes to foment unrest in Iran and encourage Iraq to continue to fight against Iran, is a negative theme with limited utility. Eventually, the leaders of the

Islamic Republic must face the realities of Iran's internal problems and try to solve them, instead of identifying the United States (primarily) as the "Great Satan." Defiance of the West has been a principal source of support for Khomeini, as it was for Nassar in Egypt and as it is for Qaddhafi in Libya. Although negative rhetoric fails to solve the internal problems of Iran, it does reinforce support for Khomeini.

President Khamene'i has stressed Iran's refusal to approach the United States to obtain advanced technology. Apparently, the United States is still considered "an oppressor, hegemonist, and imperialist power," whereas these adjectives are not used to describe the Soviet Union.[11] Foreign Minister Ali Akbar Velayati stated in mid-January 1982 that Iran will refuse to normalize relations with the United States because of U.S. support for Kurdish rebels, Marxists, and other leftist elements that oppose Khomeini. He added, however, that Iran wishes to improve its ties with the USSR, the Gulf states, and Western European countries.[12] Apparently, the Soviet Union already provides sizable aid to the Tudeh (Communist) party, while Iran "staggers on like a Rasputin, for how long no one can foresee."[13]

Khomeini has also been a proponent of the Steadfastness and Confrontation Front of Libya, Syria, and the Palestine Liberation Organization (PLO). In addition, he supports Shi'a movements throughout the world, as illustrated by the support extended to the Lebanese Shi'a Amal movement. But even here Iranian foreign policy is contradictory: although the Islamic Republic of Iran is an avowed enemy of Israel, has no diplomatic relations with it, supports the PLO, and publicly vows to liberate Jerusalem, Iran's leaders purchased arms from Israel as early as August 1980.

In order to understand the foreign policy of the Islamic Republic of Iran toward the Mideast, it is necessary, first, to examine not only the events that took place inside Iran but also Khomeini's views of the Arabs, Israel, and the PLO; and, second, to analyze the modifications in Iran's foreign policy in terms of domestic changes in Iran, Iran's involvement in the Gulf war, and Iran's isolation from the West, which resulted primarily from the seizure of the U.S. Embassy in Tehran and the detention of U.S. diplomats as hostages.

Khomeini's View: Islam and Nationalism

Iran's foreign policy since 1979 has been unconventional from the outset. The United States and the USSR have been viewed as "arch satans" and "satans" respectively. The conservative Arab leaders have been seen as "corrupt," and the West Europeans as neocolonizers and "exploiters" of Third World masses. This negative rhetoric has left Khomeini's regime little room for friendship with most of the Middle East and the West. The only possible "friends" that remained were Cuba, Syria, Libya, South Yemen, and the

Soviet/Warsaw Pact nations, plus a few nonaligned revolutionary Third World states. Khomeini views Israel as a U.S. creation and sees the United States as the principal supporter of Zionists and the so-called reactionary conservative leaders in the Middle East. He sees the Palestinians as freedom fighters who have suffered for decades from what he sees as the "expansionist" policies of Israel.

Indeed, Khomeini's weltanschauung is a simplistic view of the world, largely seen in terms of "good" and "evil," "imperialism," "Zionism," superpower "interventionism," and "exploitation." Undoubtedly, Khomeini's lifelong struggle against the Shah, his extensive residence in Iraq, and his identification with the poor Shi'a masses in Iran and Iraq have left a permanent impression on him. As the driving force behind Iran's foreign and domestic policies, however, such a worldview promotes serious problems. For example, it fosters revolutionary rhetoric that uses external powers as a scapegoat to avoid dealing with Iran's immense internal problems and to consolidate the clergy's rule by directing the Iranian Revolution toward mullahcracy.

In addition, the Islamic Republic's foreign policy has a strong moralist tone based not only on Khomeini's personal worldview, but also on Shi'a eschatology, with a strong undercurrent of Persian patriotism. Iran's adversaries are seen as satanic, both in the moralistic context of personifying "evil" and also in the broader context of the term *shaytan*, which means one who intervenes outside of his own realm of authority with malice aforethought. The product of a national political culture that began in the Safavi era (1501–1736), the Shi'a belief system emphasizes the pursuit of a righteous lifestyle, as exemplified by the life of Prophet Mohammed and Shi'a's twelve Imams. Shi'a Islam has also been shaped by Iranian history and culture. The views of the clergy have been heavily influenced by the great power rivalries in Iran, as well as by the Shah and his policies toward Israel, South Africa, and the West. Consequently, the fall of the Shah and the establishment of an Islamic Republic were accompanied by denunciations of the Shah's policies toward the United States, Israel, and South Africa.

Another general aspect of Iran's foreign policy has to do with the role of Islam and patriotism and the dilemmas they cause for Iran. That Islam and patriotism are, and will remain, the foundations of Iranian domestic and foreign policies must be recognized as the basis for understanding the forces that operate in Iran. Shi'a Islam, which evolved as the state religion and was subsequently woven into the fabric of Persian patriotism, remains the most potent unifying force in the hands of the clergy. The clergy, in turn, symbolize and personify Shi'a orthodoxy for the faithful in Iran and elsewhere. This is precisely why the Iranian Revolution is more relevant for the Shi'a than the Sunni. (The Shi'a sect differs from the Sunni sect in terms of historic differences over the rule of the early caliphs and acceptance of the validity of the *sunna.*)

In this connection, secularism, socialism, and communism—because they are imported ideologies—seem to have little appeal or relevance as models of social change and revolution in the Mideast in the 1980s, especially in comparison with Islam. Herein lies the basis of the relevance of Islamic revolution as an indigenous model of political change in the Muslim world. Although one should not overestimate the likelihood of revolutions in the Middle East based on the unique Shi'a Iranian experience, neither should one underestimate the relevance of the broad appeal of the model of Islamic revolution as an indigenous method for political change.

Because the Islamic model of revolution offers a grass-roots alternative, based on Muslim political theory, with which the masses can identify, it can provide a foundation for political legitimacy and for an acceptable relationship between those who govern and those who are governed. Unlike the rhetoric of Marxism, Leninism, the Shah's White Revolution, or Nasser's brand of socialism, with which the masses could not identify, the Islamic option can appear to be a democratic model based on Islamic socioeconomic principles. The resurgence of Islam, as illustrated and reinforced by patriotism and the upheavals in Iran, is the most important single factor influencing Iran's policy toward the rest of the Mideast. Muslim religious activism of the Iranian brand threatens most of the Mideast states. "The thing that binds Saudi Arabia and Iraq together," as Charles Ebinger has pointed out, "is fear of the spread of fundamentalist Islam out of Iran."[14]

The "threat of the Khomeini revolution" has resulted in improved relations not only between Saudi Arabia and Iraq but between Saudi Arabia and Bahrain and has reduced discord among many states of the Gulf and the Arabian Peninsula.[15] In December 1981, Saudia Arabia signed separate mutual security pacts with Bahrain and Qatar, as these two small states of the Gulf rushed to seek Saudi protection to prevent the spread of the Khomeini-style revolution in the Gulf.

Khomeini's Islamic Republic initially portended a possible resurgence of Muslim fundamentalism in the Middle East. Muslim resurgence, however, appears to be far less widespread and definitely not as violent as the Iranian case had suggested. Indeed, Iran's revolution is unique because of the evolution of Shi'a and Iranian history, an evolution that encompasses centuries of power rivalry, creating an emotionally compressed patriotic sentiment. This sentiment exploded when the Shah, with U.S. encouragement, took the lid off and then could not decide whether to use his well-known authoritarian style to clamp that lid back on.

While Islamic ideology, based on the holy Koran, pulls Iranians and Arabs together as "brethren" in Islam, the forces of patriotism, ethnicity, and culture pull them apart, particularly when there is a war between Arab Iraq and "Persian" Iran. Iran's foreign policy reflects the vicissitudes of the cohesion of Islam that binds Iranians and Arabs versus the division of Persian patriotism and pan-Arab nationalism. Indeed, the basic political structure in the Gulf states is Islamic. That is why the Shah's secularization efforts failed and why Iraqi leader Saddam Hussein's efforts to create a secular structure, without a foundation in Islam, are also bound to fail. The Saudi political system historically has been based on Islam. Islam is also the foundation of the Islamic Republic of Iran and the basis of the government in Pakistan. The smaller states of the Gulf area are also cognizant of the rising influence of Islam and have taken steps to base both their domestic and external policies on Islamic precepts.

Khomeini's alleged statement that the Persian Gulf should not be called "Persian" or "Arabian" but should be referred to as the "Islamic" Gulf can be interpreted as describing a "gulf" that distances Shi'a Iran from the Sunni Arabs. But such an evaluation would be an oversimplification, because the broader bonds of Islam usually override the Shi'a-Sunni schism. On the level of patriotism, however, what has happened in the Gulf since the fall of the Shah is, indeed, the creation of an "Islamic Gulf" in which the area's most dominant nations (Iran and Saudi Arabia) use the same scripture (the Koran) as the basis of their political legitimacy and mass support and as their source of authority. In this context, Iraq's secular brand of Arab socialism will find the Gulf region an inhospitable environment in which to thrive.

Islam is, indeed, the most virulent ideology in the Middle East today, along with patriotism. Iran's foreign policy can be viewed as the product of a dialectic between Iran's natural affinity with the Arabs and Turks as Muslim "brethren" versus the Persian patriotism and pan-Arab nationalism that distance Iran from the Arab world.

The Revolution of 1978–79: Euphoria and Reaction

In the initial phase of the revolution, many Arabs welcomed Khomeini since he interjected Iran into the politics of the Arab-Israeli dispute by breaking Iran's diplomatic relations with Egypt, renouncing Iran's ties with Israel, announcing its support for the PLO, and halting the shipment of Iranian oil to Israel. (For some time, Arab leaders had wished that the Shah would take similar actions, since he too was a Muslim leader.) Iran's relationship with Israel shifted from discreet entente to open animosity. Pars News Agency, the official press agency of Iran, stated on 18 February 1979 that the termination of all relations with Israel and the full support of the PLO were the cornerstones of Iran's foreign policy. As a result of the Egyptian-Israeli peace accord, Israel had probably written Egypt off its list of adversaries, but may have added Iran to that list. Israel was probably concerned over the new strategic development in its eastern front.

Nonetheless, conservative Arab leaders were alarmed over the appeal of Iran's model of revolution, over Iran's possible alignment with Iraq and Syria, and over the implantation of a PLO mission in Ahwaz, Iran, close to the oil fields of the lower Gulf.[16] This implantation was seen as a psychological boost for the radical Arabs and as a potential source of a major shift in favor of revolutionary forces in the Middle East. Yasir Arafat, the first foreign leader to meet with Ayatollah Khomeini in Iran, said during his February 1979 visit that Iran's Muslim revolution had "turned upside down" the balance of power in the Middle East; in turn, he received a vague pledge from the Ayatollah that Iran would "turn to the issue of victory over Israel" after the Islamic Republic consolidated its power.[17] This promise was based on Khomeini's view of the need to correct the injustices brought on the Palestinians plus the assistance of the al-Fatah branch of the PLO to Iranians prior to and during the revolution.

In this respect, al-Fatah had been involved in training Iranian revolutionaries, particularly the Mujahidin Khalq, for several years. The PLO itself supported anti-Shah elements inside and outside Iran. The Palestinians were seen in Iran as a poor, suffering people, caught in the midst of "Zionist expansionism" and "U.S. imperialism," and as a people who had been "betrayed" and neglected by centrist Arab leaders who preferred to maintain themselves in power rather than assist their oppressed Palestinian "brethren."

The severance of Iran's ties with Israel, the halt in the shipment of Iranian oil to Israel, the Islamic Republic's explicit announcement of support for the PLO, and the clergy's hope that Muslims should move toward "freeing" Jerusalem, all represented Iran's broad foreign policy rhetoric toward the Arab-Israeli dispute. In this context, the Islamic Republic was seen as a plus for the Arabs and a minus for Israel because it could tip the balance in favor of the Arabs.[18] Iran, like Libya, considered the Camp David accords as anti-Arab and anti-Palestinian. The bilateral peace treaty between Egypt and Israel was criticized by moderate and radical Arabs; West Europeans showed their skepticism toward it as the means to achieve a comprehensive peace; and the United Nations General Assembly also condemned it.[19]

Consequently, Arab sympathy for Khomeini and for the Islamic Republic of Iran was widespread in 1979. Posters of Khomeini in Palestinian camps; the general positive attitude in the Arab world toward the Iranian Revolution; and the identification of religious leaders, many students, and the poor masses with Islamic fundamentalism and revolutionary change; were viewed with a sense of pride. It was as if Iranians had miraculously joined the Arabs as Muslim brethren in the Mideast.

By the summer of 1979, however, events in Iran had changed Arab views toward Khomeini and toward the Iranian Revolution. Arabs could not comprehend the killing and other injustices that were taking place in Iran, especially since forgiveness is a cardinal principle of Islam. They thought that when the "enemy" is on his knees, as was the case with the pro-Shah generals and leaders, forgiveness should surpass murder, revenge, and "instant justice" as it was dispensed by revengeful and bloodthirsty revolutionary zealots.

In addition, specific tensions escalated between Iraq and Iran. Both states adhered to a common anti-Zionist, anti-imperialist ideology and rhetoric, tempered by each side's national interests and historical experiences. Despite these common views, the differences between the two countries surfaced quickly. Iran's leaders considered Saddam Hussein a "usurper" of power who lacked popular support and political legitimacy because the people (in the Iranian view) had yet to be allowed to openly express themselves in Iraq. Khomeini had mistakenly assumed that Iran's popular revolution could repeat itself in Iraq, without willingly recognizing that Iran was quite different from Iraq and that the forces of Arabism could unite to prevent an "Iranian" revolution in Iraq.

Iraqi leaders initially welcomed Khomeini's return to Iran in early 1979. Relations between Iran and Iraq deteriorated quickly, however, after Iran's clergy renewed their claims to Bahrain as a province of Iran and urged the Shi'a in the Gulf area to rebel against their traditional, conservative rulers, who also happened to be Sunni. By fall 1979, Shi'a demonstrations had occurred in Najaf, Iraq, in Saudi Arabia, and in Bahrain and Kuwait. These demonstrations led Saddam Hussein to warn Khomeini that "Iraq's capabilities can be used against any side which tries to violate the sovereignty of Kuwait or Bahrain or harm their people or land. This applies to the entire Gulf." Hussein also added that "the Shah occupied three Arab islands in the Gulf. If the revolution is an Islamic one, then why have they not returned the islands to their Arab owners?"[20] In October, the Iraqi ambassador in Lebanon publicly stated that Iran "should restore all Iraq's rights in Shatt al-Arab by voluntarily agreeing to amend the Algiers agreement and deal with the Iranian nationalities with a spirit . . . which rejects fanaticism and persecution."[21] These heated verbal exchanges were followed by attacks by the Pasdaran on the Iraqi Embassy in Tehran and the Iraqi Consulate in Khorramshahr, plus the occupation of Iraq's Consulate in Kermanshah. These events were followed by escalated border incidents, the hostage crisis, Bazargan's removal from office, hard-line clergy domination, and the Gulf war.

The Gulf War: Islam and Arabism

According to Claudia Wright, the fall of Mehdi Bazargan's government in November 1979, and its replacement by a revolutionary council "dominated by clerical factions, was the turning point in Iraqi-Iranian relations."[22] The removal of Bazargan and his moderate cabinet members signaled to Iraq the end of moderation and the beginning of an inflexible foreign and domestic policy dominated by the extremist, hard-line clergy who espoused subversion in Iraq and in the rest of the Gulf states. By then Saddam Hussein preferred the return of anti-Khomeini forces led by the Shah's last premier, Shahpour Bakhtiar, to replace Khomeini's regime. Iraq began to support anti-Khomeini forces in and out of Iran.

Saddam Hussein was the first Arab leader to break relations with Khomeini, to deride his regime as non-Islamic, and to say that "the Koran was written in Arabic, and God destined the Arabs (not the Iranians) to play a vanguard role in Islam."[23] Hussein's remarks not only failed to take into consideration that Islam had been greatly expanded under non-Arabs (Turks, Persians, and Berbers) but also revealed his belief that Arabs were the only true Muslims.

The Iraqi invasion of Iran on 22 September 1980—characterized by Saddam Hussein as "Qadisiyah," in reference to the Arab invasion of Persia in A.D. 637—began a chain of events that has left a deep and enduring impact on Iranian-Arab relations. Despite Iraq's initial victories in the Gulf war, the Iraqi offensive was soon halted, and Western expectations of a blitzkrieg, similar to the 1967 or 1973 Mideast wars, failed to materialize. Iraqi leaders could not maintain their successful penetration. They had underestimated the capability of the Iranian air force, the level of resistance in Iran, and the force of Iranian patriotism. By November 1980, it was clear that Saddam Hussein had failed to achieve the objectives he had hoped for. A stalemate developed in the Gulf war after November 1980, with both sides claiming to be against any compromise.

It is difficult to determine whether Hussein had, indeed, limited objectives in mind to begin with. Did he hope to gain sovereignty over a long, thin slice of the river bed in the Shatt al-'Arab estuary at a minimum, or did he seek nothing less than hegemony in the Persian Gulf? What were Ayatollah Khomeini's objectives during the war? Aside from calling the Ba'thists a "godless" regime, Khomeini wished to export the Islamic revolution, particularly to Iraq, which has a Shi'a majority ruled by a Sunni minority. Can Saddam Hussein, who has been called by his opponents "the butcher of Baghdad," last without a popular support?[24] If he fails to integrate the Kurds into the mainstream of Iraqi life, to end the war with Iran, and to win popular support among Iraq's Shi'a majority, could he survive as Iraq's leader?

Iraq is not the top candidate for stability in the Middle East. Chronic instability has characterized Iraqi politics since 1958. As Phebe A. Marr has pointed out, in the past twenty years "at least ten coups and attempted coups, two armed rebellions, and a full-scale civil war" took place in Iraq.[25] So far, the Khomeini regime has also been unstable. The Islamic revolution can be, and has been, used as a justification for the upheavals in Iran, but it is still questionable whether stability will return to Iran in the foreseeable future. As long as domestic instability prevails in Iran and Iraq, the likelihood of tension between them, in order to distract the attention of their people from domestic woes, remains high. It is precisely this linkage between domestic politics and foreign policies that has played a key role in the Gulf war.

In attacking Iran, Saddam Hussein underestimated the power of Iranian patriotism, which was reawakened as a result of the Iraqi invasion to resolidify the support of Iran's masses behind Khomeini. Saddam Hussein also underestimated Iran's military capability. Iraq won many battles in the initial phases of the Gulf war, but ultimately could well lose the contest. Such a fate appears inevitable if one considers the size, population, geography, and ideology as crucial factors in the conflict. Time also has been on Iran's side. Furthermore, the immediate dangers facing Iraq have proved greater than the threats that faced Iran. The Gulf war has unified rather than divided Iran, as Saddam Hussein may have hoped. As William O. Staudenmaier has pointed out, "What started out as Saddam's qadisiya may yet provide to be his Waterloo"[26]; indeed, it could end that way.

The Effects of the Gulf War

The small conservative states of the Gulf, Bahrain and Kuwait in particular, because of their proximity, were alarmed by the possibility that the Gulf war could spill over into their territories. This concern was further fueled by Iran's revolutionary image of Islamic fundamentalism, with which some religious ulama, students, and the poor identify. Iran's revolutionary rhetoric further heightened, and continues to heighten, the tension in the area, as illustrated by the discovery in December 1981 of the small band of revolutionaries in Bahrain dedicated to the overthrow of traditional Arab regimes. With the end of the war in sight, however, the threat of the spillover of the Gulf war is of less immediate concern. Iran could extend the war by attacking targets inside other Arab states that assisted Iraq, if Iran felt completely cornered by Iraq, or by first defeating Iraq and then extending the war into the Gulf. But these outcomes do not appear likely.

Arab states continue to denounce each other on the position each has taken on the Gulf war or on the Camp David accords. Arab differences also reflect ideological differences and their ties with the Soviet Union or the United States. During 1980, Iraq sought and created an "Arab entente," consisting of Saudi Arabia, Jordan, and some of the small Gulf sheikhdoms, to support Iraq against Iran. The support for Iraq, however, was not "without limits or conditions."[27] King Hussein deplored "collaboration" between some Arab governments and Iran against Iraq.[28] He called on Arabs to take a united stand against Iran's "crimes." The first contingent of Jordanian "volunteers" to join Iraqi troops in the Gulf war against Iran left Amman on 2 March 1982.[29] Saudi Arabia provided ample economic aid to Iraq, and Egypt sent Soviet arms through Jordan to Iraq. This increasing support for Iraq reflected the ties of Arab "brotherhood" and the reaction of the conservative Arab leaders to Khomeini's declarations to export revolution to the Arab world. Iraq's rival, Syria, supported by Libya, sided with Iran.

Libya and Syria openly supported Iran. Iraq broke diplomatic ties with Syria and Libya, while Saudi Arabia broke diplomatic ties with Libya. Indeed, one result of the Gulf war was further disunity among the Arabs who oppose the Camp David accords. Another result was to open a new wound in the Mideast, which drew attention away from the Arab-Israeli dispute. Khomeini's promise to Yasir Arafat to turn Iran's attention to the Arab-Israeli dispute distracted that attention to the Gulf war. In fact, the war and Iran's revolutionary rhetoric reduced the likelihood of a successful concentrated effort to bring peace by those who opposed the Camp David accords. The Gulf war showed the difficulties in maintaining a unified Arab stand on the Arab-Israeli dispute, let alone the achievement of a unified Muslim, Mideast stand that could include the Arabs, as well as the non-Arabs.

After the Israeli annexation of the Golan Heights, Hafiz al-Asad of Syria indicated his interest in trying to resolve the Gulf war. Damascus Radio, which expresses the official position of the Syrian government, reported on 29 December 1981 that it was time to end the Gulf war in order to conserve "Arab and Islamic energies to counter Israel's expansionist designs."[30] In reality, before Hafiz al-Asad could have mediated between Iran and Iraq, he needed to improve Syria's relations with Iraq. Reports from Kuwait indicated that then crown prince Fahd of Saudi Arabia was trying to reduce discord between Syria and Iraq, as well as between Syria and Jordan. At the same time, Saddam Hussein denounced Hafiz al-Asad's efforts toward Arab unity. In a broadcast in early January 1982, Hussein said, "He who speaks about the Zionist annexation of the Golan Heights and wants the area liberated through participation by Iraq and other Arabs must stop backing the enemies of the Arab nation."[31] Saddam Hussein was referring to Syrian support for Iran in the Gulf war. Qaddhafi, in a similar critical vein, sharply attacked Saudi Arabia. He said that the pro-American Arab states were "more dangerous than Israel and ought to be overthrown."[32]

For his part, Hafiz al-Asad also accused the United States and Iraq of providing arms and support for the Muslim Brotherhood organization in its "subversive activities" in Syria. The large-scale uprising in Hama, north of Damascus, by the Muslim Brotherhood, in which weapons manufactured in the United States and cases of arms bearing the words "property of the Government of Iraq" were found, was used by the president and secretary general of Syria's ruling Arab Socialist Ba'th party as the alleged proof of U.S. and Iraqi involvement in the Hama uprising.[33] Interestingly, Hama historically has been one of the centers of fundamentalist Muslim opposition to Asad, who seized power in a 1970 coup. The current wave of opposition has been going on since at least 1979.

Iranian and Saudi press and radio reports have continued attacks on each other since Khomeini seized power. Iranians have accused Saudi Arabia of mistreating Iranian pilgrims to Mecca and of providing military assistance to Iraq during the Gulf war. The Saudis have responded that Iranian leaders are "bringing destruction on their country and paving the way for outside intervention in the entire Gulf region."[34] "What the Iranians are doing is at variance with Islam in terms of actions, deeds, and thoughts," the Saudi daily *Okaz* stated.[35] *Al-Jazirah*, another Saudi daily, predicted in November 1981 "a hot winter for Ayatollah Khomeini and his followers," but the hot winter never materialized.

In November 1981, Khomeini denounced Prince Fahd's plan for a Mideast settlement as "inconsistent with Islam."[36] A Tehran newspaper attacked Yasir Arafat for his favorable comments toward the Saudi peace proposal. Iran and Libya were critical of Prince Fahd's plan because it implicitly suggested the recognition of Israel in return for the establishment of a state for the Palestinians. According to Pars, the official Iranian press agency, Prince Fahd's proposal "would eventually establish Israel as the master of the Islamic and Arab worlds."[37]

Since January 1982, when Tehran accused the PLO of contacting dissident Iranian leaders in France, Iranian-PLO relations have been on a downslide. Leaders of the PLO have also criticized Iran for its reported military ties with Israel.[38] According to Phil Marfleet and Edward J. Mann, "evidence is mounting that Iran is receiving arms from Israel."[39] They claimed that arms shipments from Israel to Iran "may have started even before the war began in September 1980." Apparently, a former U.S. State Department official confirmed that at least one shipment had been sent to Iran from Israel in August 1980.[40] Israeli shipments reportedly included tires for F-4 fighter bombers, parts for M-60 tanks, and an M-43 tank engine, plus engines for Scorpion tanks. These shipments may have helped turn "the tide of battle" in the Gulf war in November 1980 in favor of Iran. Former Iranian president Bani-Sadr has also confirmed the shipment of arms from Israel.

In early 1982, Khalid al-Hassan, a leading PLO official, criticized Khomeini's alleged plot in December 1981 to topple the present government in Bahrain by stating that "this irresponsible act was aimed not only at Bahrain, but at other Gulf countries...the Arab world should adopt a serious stand toward dangers menacing the Gulf."[41] Seyyed Ali Khamene'i, Iran's president, asserted that the "creation of the Bahrain problem" was aimed at diverting attention from the Israeli "annexation" of the Golan Heights. He denied that Iran had any role in the sabotage of Bahrain.[42]

Iranian leaders believe that the plight of the Palestinian people is at the core of the Mideast tragedy. In the initial phase of the revolution, Islamic leaders strongly supported the cause of Palestinians. Then, during the prolonged Gulf war, and because of the accusations of Iranian plots to overthrow the present regime in Bahrain, Iranians grew cool toward the PLO. The coolness also developed because of the reported bond between the Mujahidin Khalq led by Massoud Rajavi and the PLO; however, PLO support for Iraq was the principal factor dampening Iranian support for it. Nevertheless, the sympathy of the Iranian people still remains with the Palestinians, particularly since the June 1982 Israeli invasion of Lebanon and the subsequent massacre of Palestinians.

The Israeli bombing of Iraqi nuclear facilities on June 8, 1981, the Israeli overflight of Jordanian and Saudi air space, the Israeli bombing of civilian targets in Lebanon, the annexation of the Golan Heights, and the June 1982 invasion of Lebanon were all condemned by Iran, as were the Camp David accords and the role of the United States as an "imperialist" power in the Mideast. Over a thousand Iranians were dispatched to Lebanon as a symbol of support for the PLO, an act that was seen by the Arabs as a friendly, if ineffective, gesture.

As Robert O. Freedman has pointed out, "While in the Shah's day Iran was a key element of the American anti-Soviet alliance grouping, today it is a major factor preventing the formation of the anti-imperialist Arab unity which Moscow has been seeking."[43] In reality, the Gulf war has increased the differences between Arabs who oppose the Camp David accords and reduced the chances of the conservative Arab states to gain support for various initiatives that would begin the process as a comprehensive settlement of the Arab-Israeli dispute.

Conclusions

Iran's anti-Soviet, anti-U.S., and anti-Israeli rhetoric since the Shah's ouster has not succeeded in the Middle East. So far, Iran's foreign policy toward the Middle East has accomplished none of the objectives of toppling conservative, pro-Western regimes, supporting the Palestinian cause, or "freeing" Jerusalem. Khomeini's words and actions, however, did contribute to the outbreak of the Gulf war, which has created a new crisis in Mideast politics and could leave a deep scar in Iran's relations with the Arabs.

Saddam Hussein's precipitous decision to invade Iran proved to be the biggest blunder he has ever made. It was an opportunistic overreaction to Iran's revolutionary upheavals. Khomeini's rhetoric of exporting the Islamic revolution has also proved to be a blunder in the conduct of Iran's foreign policy. In a broader sense, however, the revolutionary zeal of extremists in Iran in the first phase of the revolution is probably typical of any genuine revolution, as is the overreaction of Iraq's leaders, who were alarmed at the possibility of a revolution in their country.

The main event influencing Iran's policy toward the Arab world has been the Gulf war. It is to be hoped that Khomeini now realizes that Arab ties supersede Muslim ties and that, in the final analysis, Iran, as a non-Arab state, cannot gain support when it is involved in a war against an Arab state. These political realities should have a sobering impact on the clergy in Iran and could change its revolutionary rhetoric toward the Mideast. But it is more likely that the hostility of Tehran toward the conservative, centrist Arab regimes will continue for as long as Khomeini is alive or his policies are pursued. In the absence of Khomeini, Iran could possibly remain dedicated to the export of revolution or might moderate its policy in that respect. As long as Iran is dedicated to exporting revolution and fomenting Shi'a unrest in the Mideast, however, Arab-Iranian relations will remain cool. When the Gulf war finally ends, perhaps Iran will moderate its extremist rhetoric, and its relations with the Arabs could improve.

Iran's foreign policy failures in the Middle East since the Camp David accords illustrate Khomeini's inflexible and dogmatic view based on his desire to export revolution. These failures also illustrate his naive views of the foreign policy and defense challenges that Iran faces, in its location directly below the Soviet Union, in an area of potential superpower conflict, and between two zones of conflict, the Arab-Israeli and the Indo-Pakistani.

Being a religious leader, with his own vision of how to ensure that the government acts in accordance with Islam *(velayate faghih)*, Khomeini sees it as his religious duty to attempt to export the Islamic revolution to the Middle East, without regard for the consequences of his exhortations. Herein lies the heart of Iran's foreign policy problems. The pro-Khomeini clergy has chosen to disregard the former Shah's astute evaluation of Iran's role in the framework of political realities of East-West rivalry, Arab-Israeli conflict, Shi'a-Sunni cleavages, and Persian versus pan-Arab nationalism. Khomeini has ignored all these complex issues in favor of his preferences as to what should be, rather than what are, the political realities in the Middle East. As long as this trend continues, Iran will remain a source of tension and instability in the Gulf area and in the entire Mideast.

Notes

1. John Kifner, "Iran Pursues Grim Repression to Meet Guerillas' Challenge," *New York Times*, 18 January 1981, p. 1.

2. James A. Bill, "Power and Religion in Revolutionary Iran," *Middle East Journal* 36 (1982): 22.

3. William B. Quandt, "The Middle East Crises," *Foreign Affairs* 58 (1979/80): 545–46.

4. Eric Rouleau, "Khomeini's Iran," *Foreign Affairs* 59 (1980/81): 19.

5. R. K. Ramazani, "Who Lost America? The Case of Iran," *Middle East Journal* 36, no. 1 (Winter 1982): 7.

6. Kifner, "Iran Pursues Grim Repression."

7. Foreign Broadcast Information Service *(FBIS)*, 7 January 1982, p. i.

8. Ibid., 8 January 1982, p. ii.

9. Ibid., 11 January 1982, p. i.

10. Ramazani, "Who Lost America?" p. 21.

11. *FBIS, Middle East and Africa*, 8 January 1982, p. ii.

12. Ibid., 13 January 1982), p. ii.

13. Barry Rubin, "US Aid for Pakistan," *New York Times*, 19 February 1982, p. A31.

14. "Iraq's Ambitious War Aims," *Newsweek*, 6 October 1981, p. 38.

15. "Syria, in Bid to End Iran-Iraq War, Seeks Talks with Teheran," *New York Times*, 30 December 1981, p. A3.

16. James M. Markham, "Arafat, in Iran, Reports Khomeini Pledges Aid for Victory over Israel," ibid., 19 February 1979, p. 1.

17. Ibid.

18. Robert G. Darius, "The Iranian Revolution of 1978–79: Potential Implications for Major Countries in the Area," in Enver M. Koury and Charles G. MacDonald, eds., *Revolution in Iran: A Reappraisal* (Washington, D.C.: Institute of Middle Eastern and North African Affairs, 1982), pp. 30–48.

19. Abba Eban, "The Saudi Text," *New York Times*, 18 November 1981, p. A31.

20. As quoted by Claudia Wright in "Implications of the Iraq-Iran War," *Foreign Affairs* 59 (1980/81): 278.

21. Ibid.

22. Ibid., p. 279.

23. Claudia Wright, "Iraq—New Power in the Middle East," *Foreign Affairs* 58 (1979/80): 260.

24. "Iraq's Ambitious War Aims," *Newsweek*, 6 October 1981, p. 37.

25. Phebe A. Marr, "The Political Elite in Iraq," in George Lenczowski, ed., *Political Elites in the Middle East* (Washington, D.C.: American Enterprise Institute for Public Policy Research, 1975), p. 125.

26. William O. Staudenmaier, "A Strategic Analysis of the Gulf War" (Carlisle Barracks, Penn.: U.S. Army War College, Strategic Studies Institute, n.d.), p. 31.

27. Wright, "Implications," p. 285.

28. *FBIS, Middle East and Africa*, 7 January 1982, p. i.

29. "Jordanian Volunteers Leave for Iraq," *New York Times*, 3 March 1982, p. A5.

30. "Syria, in Bid to End Iran-Iraq War, Seeks Talks with Teheran," p. A3.

31. "New Denunciations Hinder Arab Efforts on Unity," ibid., 8 January 1982, p. A3.

32. Ibid.

33. "Syria's Chief Says US Sends Arms to Insurgents," ibid., 8 March 1982, p. A3.

34. "Khomeini Rules out Saudis' Peace Plan as Contrary to Islam," ibid., 18 November 1981, p. A13.

35. Ibid.

36. Ibid.

37. Ibid.

38. "Alleged Iranian-Backed Plot Criticized by PLO Official," *Saudi Report* 3 (1 February 1982): 9.

39. Phil Marfleet and Edward J. Mann, "Seeking Arms from the Devil," *Middle East Magazine* 87 (January 1982): 20.

40. Ibid.

41. "Alleged Iranian-Backed Plot Criticized by PLO Official," p. 9.

42. *FBIS, Middle East and Africa*, 8 January 1982, p. ii.

43. Robert O. Freedman, "Soviet Policy Toward Khomeini's Iran: A Preliminary Analysis" (unpublished paper, n.d.), p. 45.

4 | The Iraq-Iran War:
Conflict, Linkage, and Spillover in the Middle East

John W. Amos, II

Discussions of conflict in the Middle East usually revolve around the Arab-Israeli conflict. While this particular conflict clearly has the potential of escalating into wars of increasing scope and destructiveness, it is by no means the only conflict in the area. Rather, it is the most visible of a series of conflicts that crosscut the region and shape its political dynamics. The war between Iraq and Iran illustrates both the inherently unstable nature of the political environment and the prevailing pattern of conflict linkages in the Middle East.[1]

The war, which began in 1980, is a greatly expanded version of a pattern of intermittent fighting between the two states. This fighting, in turn, is the product of a long-standing territorial dispute over demarcation of the border and right of access to the Shatt al-'Arab, the estuary at the head of the Gulf. Its origins lie in the politics and diplomacy of the breakup of the Ottoman empire at the turn of the century. Each side has, however, extended the conflict by strategic design to encompass reciprocal claims to the loyalties of Kurdish, Arab, and Shi'ite communities residing within the other country. Regionally, both sides have extended the strategic rivalry for control to the Gulf itself and made claims on the territories of various Gulf states. Both sides, again by conscious design, have expanded the conflict to include much more extensive

The views, opinions, and/or findings contained in this report are those of the author and should not be construed as an official Department of the Navy position, policy, or decision.

configurations of both Middle Eastern (and some non–Middle Eastern) states and cross-national communities located outside the two states.

Because of its protracted and militarily inconclusive nature, the war has forced both sides to engage in extensive coalition-building strategies to secure the political and military resources necessary to continue fighting. The trade-offs and linkages generated in the course of implementing these strategies enmeshed the original Iraq Iran conflict in still other conflicts. Consequently, the continued fighting has energized a pattern of conflict linkages throughout the Middle East and created a causal chain of violence, which has broken out in areas at some distance from the scene of actual military operations. For example, Shi'a uprisings against Sunni ruling elites in a number of countries can, in part, be traced to tensions arising from the Iraq-Iran conflict. Sunni violence directed at both Shi'as and Christians, in part again, is attributable to the war. These linkages, however, are neither straightforward in terms of a direct causal relationship nor sequential in terms of a simple chronological order. Rather the pattern of conflict linkages is one involving both independent actions spontaneously triggered by events elsewhere and calculated political and organizational ties. The net effect is that violence in the Iraq-Iran context has frequently spilled over into other parts of the Middle East.

A Multidimensional Conflict System

Even though Middle Eastern conflicts and outbursts of violence may appear sporadic and discontinuous, there are some clearly discernible connections. These connections arise from the interaction of strategies of conflict pursued by various national and non-national actors. The structure of conflicts or, alternatively, the structure of "threats" facing the strategists in question determines the parameters of these strategies. For example, the Iraqi decision to attack Iran in September 1980 was a calculated response to a policy environment dominated by a series of interlocking conflicts. Iraq decided on war in an almost Clausewitzian fashion, after a pragmatic consideration of all options available.[2] The subsequent Iraqi strategy of conflict was an extension of this calculation.

The prewar situation facing Iraqi policymakers was one of extreme uncertainty, a situation in which pre-existing sources of threat seemed to be intensifying and thereby becoming increasingly less susceptible to Iraqi strategies of conflict management. In short, time was running out for the Iraqis in late 1980: the emergence of a revolutionary government in Iran had added a new and dangerously unpredictable element in a conflict-ridden environment that was already only marginally tolerable. The Iraqi need to respond to this environment, to create a set of defensive coalitions or to engage in pre-emptive war, is but one example of a dominant theme in contemporary Middle Eastern politics.[3]

Although the 22 September 1980 attack was a specific response to a pattern of events that Iraqi leaders perceived as moving toward an unacceptable conclusion, it is possible to identify a larger and more stable configuration of factors influencing both Iraqi and other decision makers in the Middle East. Here some of the notions from formal conflict theory may prove to be useful. Too often Middle Eastern politics is analyzed in the terminology of balance-of-power theories—theories basically drawn from and adapted to Western experience. In this usage, attention focuses on the calculus of strategy: on rational responses to perceived conflicts. This model of interaction is applicable to Middle Eastern politics, but it by no means comprehends the complexity of political action in the area. Other modes of conflict, other patterns of decision making, should be taken into account.

In this regard, theorists of conflict have advanced a number of classificatory schemes. The common assumption underlying these schemes is that each social or cultural unit or combination has an associated pattern of conflict. That is to say, conflicts between states are characterized by one pattern of conflict, while conflicts between substate communities are characterized by another. More important, different levels or types of conflict can be ranked in terms of the size and nature of the units involved. Theoretically, a model of conflict behavior can conceivably identify layers of conflict of successively broader scope and with greater levels of potential violence.[4]

Along these lines, at least three sources or levels of conflict (in addition to conflict at the state or balance-of-power level) can be identified: (1) intracommunal conflicts, which are basically conflicts between individuals, cliques, factions, or party organizations that grow out of small group or kinship structures; (2) intercommunal conflicts, which are larger and more inclusive conflicts between ethnic and other such groups that originate in the relations of various primordial communities, however defined; and, (3) intracultural conflicts, which are more pervasive conflicts between value systems that occur between religiously defined communities.[5] Therefore, a model (if it is to be useful at all in explaining Middle Eastern politics) must not only consider rationally conducted balance-of-power conflicts, but also conceptually describe the multiplicity of nonstate conflicts.

The Strategic Level: Conflict and Geopolitics

In strategic terms, the givens of Iraq's geopolitical position impelled some action, especially in response to a threat to Iraqi security interests in the Gulf. Claudia Wright has cogently analyzed Iraq's strategic vulnerability:

For Iraq, the Shatt al Arab is only one of its geographic vulnerabilities in the area. Another feature of the map is that, between Fao and Umm Qasr, Iraq has less than 50 miles of coastline on the Gulf—most of it unusable for shipping. The main port, Basra, is nearly twice that distance away from the Gulf, up the Shatt al Arab, and even in the best of times it has a three-month cargo bottleneck. Umm Qasr, the Iraqi naval base, lies on the border with Kuwait, and can only be reached by sea through a narrow passage between the Iraqi shore and Kuwaiti islands. The approach to Fao and the entrance to the Shatt estuary is commanded by Iranian artillery and naval posts on and around Abadan Island.

From the Iraqi point of view, hostile hands are always potentially around the country's throat. Like Jordan at the Gulf of Aqaba, Iraq at the Persian Gulf must share its access to the sea with a non-Arab state and traditional enemy. Iraq is also the only member of OPEC (the Organization of Petroleum Exporting Countries) whose oil exports cannot reach the outside world without crossing foreign territory in the north (Syria, Lebanon and Turkey), or without coming so close to Iranian territory in the south that it cannot be said to enjoy territorial security at all for its principal means of survival.[6]

This vulnerability, then, stemmed from a geopolitical encirclement. Iraq's neighbors to the north and east, Turkey, Syria, and Iran, were either hostile (Syria and Iran) or unable to prevent the transit of military supplies to internal and external opponents of the Iraqi regime (Turkey).[7] The consequence was not only a heightened Iraqi perception of isolation and impending threat to security, but also a corresponding Iraqi impulse to pre-empt, either politically or militarily.[8] Iraqi president Saddam Hussein himself attests to the accuracy of Wright's analysis. Speaking to the nation after the outbreak of war, Hussein stated, with some justification, that the *casus belli* was the Iranian threat to cut Iraqi access to the Gulf:

When the competent Iraqi authorities began to apply the measures of sovereignty over Shatt al-'Arab—measures of a completely peaceful nature—the Iranian authorities opened fire on the Iraqi and foreign ships passing through it. They also directly attacked our civilian targets and economic installations in the Shatt al-'Arab and Basra city regions. This act meant complete suspension of international navigation in Shatt al-'Arab and the cutting off of the vital vein of Iraq's economy. Iran has shore along the gulf extending for hundreds of kilometers, while Iraq has only limited outlets, most important of which is Shatt al-'Arab.

This decision by the Iranian authorities meant war. Iran followed this up by closing the airspace between Iran and the states in the region. This behavior clearly meant preparation for launching a war. They began with an airstrike against Iraq. Their massing of troops on the front and the information we received before and during the battles absolutely confirmed that the Iranian authorities had intended to launch war against Iraq.[9]

The Intracultural Level: Conflict and Religion

Here the central issue was the loyalty of the Shi'a community in Iraq. Socially, these Shi'a had never been fully integrated into Iraqi society. They had maintained their own social order, and, more important, they had maintained an embryonic political structure under the leadership of the Shi'ite clergy.[10] Conflict between this community and the predominantly Sunni government remained latent until the late 1970s. Prior to that time, Shi'a leaders had avoided any direct political confrontation. Shi'a hostility that did surface was sublimated into support for the Iraqi Communist party. However, in response to a more general Islamic trend in the area, Shi'a militancy percolated to the surface in a series of riots in 1977. The riots themselves were largely an amorphous and spontaneous expression of Shi'a discontent arising out of their relatively disadvantaged social position in Iraq.[11] But there were also indications of both Iranian and Syrian organizational and propaganda efforts.

Evidence of this outside intervention convinced the regime that internal security could well be jeopardized by cross-border contacts, especially contacts mediated by an extensive cross-national infrastructure based on Shi'a *husseiniyyah*s ("community centers" where the Shi'a faithful gather to study religious texts).[12] This husseiniyyah structure was supplemented and given a specifically political orientation by a fundamentalist Shi'a party known as al-Da'wah (The Call.) According to Iraqi spokesman, al-Da'wah members were responsible for fomenting unrest within the Shi'a community.[13] Iranian organizers were complemented by a somewhat less formidable, but no less dangerous, network of Syrian-organized Shi'a cells both in the Shi'a community and in the Ba'th party itself.[14] In addition, the Syrians backed the Movement of Islamic Revolution in Iraq, an organization with links to Khomeini supporters in Qom.

The Intercommunal Level: Conflict and Primordialism

There were two other major sources of opposition to the regime. The first of these was the Kurdish community to the north, which had extensive links with Kurds in Iran and Turkey and a tradition of opposition to Baghdad.[15] Kurdish insurgency had escalated during the 1960s, and when the Ba'th took power in 1968, it confronted an ongoing rebellion in the north. Over the years, Kurdish guerrilla forces, collectively known as the Pesh Merga,[16] had been able to take advantage of the mountainous terrain to prevent Iraqi forces from controlling large areas in the north. From their enclaves, Kurdish units even managed to attack some northern cities. The insurgency developed into a cyclical pattern of Iraqi summer offensives, followed by a lull in the fighting during the winter and by renewed fighting as soon as the weather permitted the Iraqis to employ their armor and aircraft.

This uneasy military stalemate persisted until 1974–1975 when Kurdish leaders, for some unaccountable reason, switched from their traditional hit-and-run tactics to fighting a conventional-style war against Iraqi mechanized units. As a result, Iraqi forces with heavy air, armor, and artillery support were able to drive Kurdish forces back in many areas and break up their organizational structure.[17] Kurdish military opposition collapsed and apparently ended, especially after 1975 when the Shah (and the United States) withdrew support.[18] The nucleus of the Kurdish insurgent movement, however, was left intact, and a number of clandestine Kurdish guerrilla organizations remained. The potential for another full-fledged Kurdish uprising still existed.[19]

The Intracommunal Level: Conflict and Organization

The remaining threat to the regime derived from the organizational capability of the Iraqi Community party (ICP). The ICP, one of the oldest and best organized of the Arab communist parties, was active both in the Kurdish north and the Shi'a south. Its organizational structure was capable of linking and mobilizing both Shi'a and Kurdish opposition. Although the ICP itself represented a conflict that stemmed from a narrow organizational base (a conflict rooted in group structure and dynamics), its ability to tie in other conflicts made it a formidable opponent. The Iraqi government responded by attempting to destroy the ICP's organizational structure. Since 1976, most ICP leaders had either been killed or forced to flee, but much of the party's organizational structure remained intact. A number of ICP cadres were still operating, and these had ties with the Syrians, the Palestinians, Iranian Communists, and even the Libyans.[20]

Strategy and Counterstrategy: Linkage and Sequence

As a result of these overlapping conflicts, a complex pattern of strategic interaction developed. The basic strategic goal of domestic opponents of the Iraqi government was to secure arms and financing from bordering states. Kurdish, Shi'a, and communist groups sought aid from Syria and Iran, as well as from more distant suppliers. In turn, the Syrians and Iranians utilized a strategy of exploiting divisions within Iraq to prevent Iraq from devoting its resources to its border conflicts with Syria and Iran. At various times, the Syrians supplied aid to Kurdish insurgents in the north,[21] to Shi'a militants to the south,[22] and to the ICP.[23] The Iranians followed a similar pattern. The bulk of arms and supplies reaching Kurdish forces came from Iran. Shi'a militants also received covert Iranian assistance. (As early as September 1974, the

Iranians had begun sending agents to propagandize among Iraqi Shi'a.) Syrian and Iranian strategy here was to force the Iraqis to split their resources and deal with domestic threats in the south as well as the north.[24]

Iraqi counterstrategy was twofold: to seal off border areas and thus deprive domestic opponents of outside sources of supply and, in a larger sense, to create a coalition of support in a wider circle of states in order to outflank those states aiding its opponents. On the borders, the Iraqis engaged in harassing tactics against Kurdish enclaves in both Iran and Turkey. Iraqi aircraft deliberately bombed Kurdish villages in Iran and Turkey, and Iraqi troops skirmished with Iranian and Turkish forces. This strategy worked along the Turkish borders. In 1974 the Turks closed their borders to Kurdish insurgents, and the Iraqis were able to set up a twenty-kilometer-wide buffer zone emptied of population and patrolled by Iraqi troops. The Iranians, however, responded differently; they escalated their aid to the Kurds and massed troops on the border.

By 1974 the Iraqis decided that something more was needed to deprive the Kurds of arms and supplies and, conversely, that their own resources needed to be increased. In particular, it was necessary for the Iraqis to break out of their virtual isolation in the Arab world. This isolation was a result of their extreme ideological orientation coupled with their extensive use of international terrorism against the regimes and leaders of the area. Iraqi strategy orientation and policy energy shifted outward toward a larger concentric circle of states in the Arab world.

During 1974 Saddam Hussein visited Algeria, Libya, and Turkey in an effort to counter the Egyptian-Saudi axis that emerged during and after the 1973 war. The Iraqis also worked to counterbalance increasing tension with Iran, the PLO, and Syria and to mitigate the potential impact of a recently established anti-Ba'thist regime in North Yemen on Iraqi ambitions in the Gulf.[25] They also made efforts to reach a modus vivendi with the Turks concerning common border problems, especially those connected with the control of Kurdish separatist activities originating on either side of the border.[26]

By contrast, Syria had been hostile since the late 1960s when the two Ba'thist regimes became rivals for leadership of the Ba'th movement and the Arab world.[27] In 1966 the Syrians had managed to expel Saddam Hussein and Ahmad Hasan al-Bakr (later the first Ba'thist president of Iraq) from the Ba'th National Command. When al-Bakr and Hussein took over in Iraq in 1968, they in turn created a rival National Command in Baghdad and staffed it with Syrian exiles. By 1976 this rivalry had degenerated into open confrontation over the distribution of water from the Euphrates, and both sides mobilized forces along the border.[28] The crisis was de-escalated, but open military confrontation was replaced by surrogate warfare. Syrian and Iraqi "hit teams" planted bombs and engaged in assassinations.[29] The short-lived Syrian-Iraqi rapprochement of 1978 was only a temporary exception to this pattern of confrontation.

The Iraqis supplemented this concentric geopolitical approach with a strategy of dealing with each opponent individually and sequentially. In 1974 and 1975, Iraqi military and political attention focused on the Kurds. After the 1975 Algiers agreement and subsequent treaty with Iran, most of the Kurdish sources of supply dried up. Iraqi forces were able to inflict heavy losses on the Kurds, driving most of their leaders into exile, along with 200,000 refugees, and capturing large amounts of arms.[30] Iraqi attention then turned to the ICP, and its leadership was decimated by a series of arrests and by the execution of a number of ICP leaders in 1976. Later, Baghdad augmented this direct attack by organizing the Iraqi Communist Vanguards as a counter-organization to draw off potential recruits from the ICP.

By 1979, however, a new combination of internal and external threats had upset this complex strategy. This combination seemed to require the use of a military option; namely, an attack on Iran. Iraq decided on war in August 1979, a little over a year before the attack[31] and apparently almost immediately after then president al-Bakr was forced to abdicate in favor of Hussein in July 1979. Behind the decision was an immediate need to stabilize the regime on three fronts:

1. To secure the loyalty of the military, as well as of the civilian bureaucracy, both of which had been demoralized by purges. One of Saddam Hussein's first moves was to raise the pay of the military and expand other allowances and social benefits.[32] Allowing the military to plan and then execute an attack was basically an extension of this strategy (a strategy used by President Anwar Sadat to secure the loyalty of key personnel in the Egyptian military prior to the 1973 war).

2. To create an immediate alliance to counter a sudden and unexpected threat from Syria—the alleged personal involvement of Syrian president Hafiz al-Asad in an attempted coup that precipitated Saddam Hussein's take over.[33] The Syrian involvement created a "personal war" between Hussein and Asad and resulted in an abrupt switch in Iraqi policy toward Syria.[34] In practice this switch meant opposing Syrian policies and alliances in the region, backing Sunni opponents of the Syrian regime, and cooperating with Jordan to outflank Syria geographically.

3. To deal with the increasingly hostile regime of Khomeini, a hostility that was especially threatening because Khomeini commanded the support of most Iraqi Shi'a. Relations between the Iraqi government and Khomeini had been relatively neutral during the ten years of Khomeini's exile at Najaf in Iraq prior to autumn of 1978. This was principally because any differences that had surfaced were subordinated to a larger common opposition to the Shah. Even so, by October 1978 these differences had reached a point where Khomeini

had decided to leave Najaf for Paris.[35] According to versions circulated in Shi'a circles, Khomeini had been forced to choose between leaving or staying in Iraq under virtual house arrest isolated from his followers.[36]

Even before Khomeini left for Paris, both Iraq and Saudi Arabia had become increasingly worried about the spread of militant Shi'ism in the Gulf area and had moved toward a common policy of blocking it.[37] As early as November 1978, at the time of the Baghdad Summit, they had agreed on a joint policy for containing Iranian-sponsored violence.[38] Iraqi and Saudi leaders had also concluded that it was in their mutual interests to back the Shah against the increasing Shi'a violence, although the Iraqis saw the Shah as the least objectionable leader for Iran.[39]

The shift from a conservative Iranian opponent to a revolutionary one was especially destabilizing insofar as the Iraqis were concerned. The Shah, for all his military power, had remained a conservative force in the area. His ability to appeal to wider circles of Arab states and cross-national actors was relatively limited. Khomeini's Islamic republic ideology, however, had tremendous appeal to Shi'a throughout the area.[40] After Khomeini's takeover in Iran in February 1979, relations between Iraq and the new Iranian regime deteriorated rapidly. By midsummer, Iranian religious leaders associated with Khomeini had openly asserted, or reasserted, traditional Iranian claims to Bahrain and had called on Shi'ites in the Gulf states to rebel.[41]

The potential Shi'ite unrest extended even to Saudi Arabia. By October 1979, Riyadh had mobilized troops to forestall possible Shi'a uprisings in the al-Hasa Province and instituted security measures in the Hijaz.[42] Nevertheless, Islamic insurgents seized the Grand Mosque at Mecca in November and held out against Saudi security forces for about two weeks.[43]

The call to rebellion had affected religious communities in the Gulf as well as those at some distance from Iraq. Shi'a violence extended to the United Arab Emirates (UAE), Kuwait, and India.[44] Other religious riots took place in Turkey, Pakistan, and Bangladesh, which heightened governmental fears of a general Islamic uprising throughout the area,[45] especially because this violence appeared to be a response to Khomeini's call for revolt against these regimes.[46] About the same time, Iraqi intelligence claimed to have discovered extensive links between Khomeini followers in Iraq and Syrian Shi'ites.[47] According to Hussein, the Syrian embassy was the center of a plot to poison the water system of Najaf and Karbala and trigger a large-scale Shi'a uprising.[48]

The newly installed Khomeini government began to supply the Kurdish Democratic party (KDP) with arms, financial aid, and supplies.[49] This revitalized Kurdish activity triggered Iraqi reprisals and, beginning in early 1980, border clashes. These escalated in midsummer 1980, and at one point there were reports of Iraqi troops being massed not only on the border with Iran, but also on the Syrian border.

In a parallel development, the remnant of the ICP set up a politburo-in-exile in Beirut in May 1979. At the same time, the party began to reorganize itself in Iraq, and leaders of the ICP extended their contacts with Kurdish opponents of the regime. This new cooperation later took the form of joint communist-Kurdish attacks on Iraqi installations during the war.[50]

By August 1979, Iraqi leaders faced several sources of threat, which were becoming more menacing and at the same time coalescing. In response, the Iraqis adopted a strategy of conflict that would allow them to dispatch all of these opponents. Iraqi military forces would attack the main opponent—Iran—which seemed to be especially vulnerable. At the same time, this war would be used as a basis to call for national unity and to legitimate attacks against domestic dissidents.[51] By late August 1980, border skirmishing had escalated into heavy artillery duels and exchanges of air strikes.[52] Iraqi forces began crossing into Iranian territory to attack Iranian positions between 7 and 13 September, before the major ground attack.[53]

The Orchestration of Conflict: Strategy for a Limited War

After the outbreak of the war, Western military strategists immediately predicted an easy victory for Iraqi forces. The Iraqis, they said, should be able to take advantage of Iranian military disorder to score a "blitzkrieg-like" success along the lines of that carried out by Israeli forces in 1967. When this did not happen and it became evident that the Iraqis were proceeding with extreme caution, Western analysts began predicting disaster for the Iraqis. The Iraq-Iran war, they now said, offered little in the way of "lessons" for the West concerning the pattern of warfare in the Third World.[54] While this interpretation may be correct from a technical military point of view, it missed the point. From the perspective of conflict and linkage theory,[55] the Iraqi strategy of limited war was a calculated attempt to exploit certain conflict patterns while minimizing others.[56]

From the beginning, the Iraqis conducted the war in line with a well-thought-out military and political strategy (not unlike the strategy adopted by the Egyptians and Syrians in 1973).[57] Iraqi planners had expended considerable energy in planning the offensive, drawing up detailed plans covering all aspects of the projected fighting. The plans included ways to mobilize psychologically and physically Iraqi manpower resources and gave careful attention to the creation of a logistics base capable of supporting a prolonged war.[58] The planners took into account civil defense considerations as well as the creation of the Popular Army, a militia of young people designed to assume internal security functions to permit the transfer of regular forces to the front.[59]

The timing of the attack was based on a number of assessments concerning the relative weakness of the Iranians. Politically, the Iranians were isolated from any potential U.S. support because of the hostage crisis. The Iranians were equally isolated from the Arab world. Moreover, the Iraqis had built up a coalition of Arab support for any move against the Iranians. In this connection, Baghdad apparently secured the particularly important support of Saudi Arabia (including specific Saudi approval of the proposed attack) during a meeting between Hussein and King Khalid at Ta'if in early August 1980. Other leaders critical to Iraqi plans who had been informed were King Hussein of Jordan, King Hassan of Morocco, French president Giscard d'Estaing,[60] and the heads of a number of the Gulf states.[61]

This coalition was the product of considerable prewar Iraqi diplomacy. After the Baghdad Summit of 1978, the Iraqis had deliberately assumed the role of moderates in Arab politics. Hussein expanded this role by promulgating the Arab Charter in early 1980. The charter stated a series of principles that were to guide Iraqi foreign policy, among them a renunciation of the use of force in intra-Arab matters.[62] On the basis of this new definition of Iraq's role in the area, Iraqi strategists were able to utilize the security concerns of the Gulf states to create an enlarged version of the original Iraqi-Saudi axis. This expanded alliance, known as the Baghdad Group, consisted of the Gulf states, Iraq, Saudi Arabia, and Morocco linked by a series of overlapping security arrangements aimed at countering potential Soviet and Iranian threats.[63]

In addition, Iraqi strategists counted on two factors to limit any swift and massive Iranian military deployment to meet an attack. On the one hand, Soviet activities in Afghanistan posed a threat that would force the Iranians to keep at least part of their forces in the eastern part of the country. On the other hand, the Iranian regime itself was obviously having difficulties asserting its legitimacy and could well be expected to react to any attack in a disorganized manner.

Some very specific military assessments also influenced the timing of the attack. Iraqi intelligence (along with a number of Western intelligence services)[64] apparently thought that Iranian forces would be in no condition to fight due to extensive purges in the officer corps, disruption of training, and disorganization of maintenance and logistics facilities.[65] According to Arab sources, the senior officer corps had been decimated, as officers closely connected with the Shah fled for their lives. Desertions in some units ran as high as 60 percent of the remaining officers and men.[66] It was suspected that the surviving officer corps was covertly hostile to the Khomeini regime and, consequently, relations between the government and its military were extremely tense. The then president, Abolhasan Bani-Sadr, later admitted that the purges had been a serious mistake because of the near disastrous consequences for Iranian military effectiveness.[67] The ground forces suffered most from the purges. According to Bani-Sadr, 10,000 of the 12,000 military personnel purged were from the army. Only one regular army division was available to meet the initial Iraqi attack; other units were considered to be too weakly organized to withstand Iraqi firepower.[68]

The Iraqis also expected the Iranian air force to be nearly useless. Many of its pilots had either fled or were imprisoned. Spare parts were scarce, and the Iranian technicians that were available were cannibalizing their planes for parts in order to keep some aircraft operational.[69] Given this information, Iraqi planners expected their ground forces to advance unhindered by Iranian air attacks.

The Iraqis had been aided in their planning by intelligence passed along by expatriate senior Iranian officers. These were clustered around Shahpour Bakhtiar's National Iranian Resistance Movement, which was headquartered in Paris. Expatriate officers had ties with others remaining in Iran and, on the basis of these ties, had informed the Iraqis that organization and morale among the Iranian military forces were so bad that they would collapse at once in the face of a determined Iraqi attack. If this did not occur, the ensuing chaos could be used as an opportunity for the expatriates to stage a coup.[70]

Iraqi planners also counted on the activities of Kurdish insurgents in the north to draw off Iranian military forces from the south. In preparation, the Iraqi army had trained anti-Iranian Kurdish forces. Although the Iraqis later claimed that Kurdish forces fought independently of Iraqi control,[71] they had apparently given considerable thought to the use of these forces.[72] Both before and during the war, Kurdish insurgents were active in the areas around Sanandaj and Mahabad in northwestern Iran.

Finally, the Iraqis expected the Arab populations in southern Iran to revolt. Part of the original invasion plan called establishing a military government in these areas and their eventual detachment from Iran under the aegis of an extension of the Iraqi Ba'thist party organization.[73] This plan was predicated on the existence of several anti-Iranian groups that had been receiving Iraqi arms and other support for at least a year prior to the attack. Indeed, as early as July 1979, Arab sources reported that the Iraqis were considering a military thrust into Khuzistan/Arabistan to create a "liberated zone" some twelve to twenty miles deep, which would include the city of Khorramshahr. This enclave would then function as a staging base for further guerrilla operations in southern Iran; Khorramshahr (renamed al-Muhammara, its original Arabic name) would act as an "Arab Hanoi."[74] In the summer of 1979, several of these groups had coordinated their efforts and fought with Iranian police and military. The difficulties that the Iranians had in quelling this insurrection apparently led Iraqi intelligence to conclude that it could be repeated on a much larger scale with Iraqi military help. To this end, a "free Arabistan" organization, which consisted of a coalition of various Arab groups in the rear, was organized under Iraqi auspices in midsummer 1981.[75]

These estimates proved wrong. Purges in the Iranian military appear to have affected mostly senior officers; middle-echelon and junior officer cadres were left largely intact. These provided a sufficient command structure to enable Bani-Sadr and his staff to deploy Iranian forces against the Iraqis. Enough trained pilots were available, and these were able to perform effectively (some pilots were apparently released from prison to fly air strikes). Maintenance in the Iranian air force was not as poor as expected; over half of its planes were able to take part in combat.[76] These Iranian pilots proved more than able to engage their Iraqi counterparts. The military did not rebel, and the projected organizational collapse did not occur. In addition, Revolutionary Guard units, whose military effectiveness was an unknown quantity at the war's start, fought with particular ferocity. Their house-to-house defense of key cities in the Shatt al-'Arab complex forced the Iraqis into a bypass and siege strategy rather than a quick capture.[77]

Perhaps most unexpected was the rapid reaction of the Iranian military. On the first day of the Iraqi attack, Iranian aircraft immediately responded by bombing Iraqi targets. On the ground, however, Iranian forces were severely outnumbered and outgunned.[78] A major portion of available army units were tied down fighting Kurdish insurgents to the north (as correctly foreseen by Iraqi intelligence), and the absence of these units greatly hampered the ability of the Iranian defenders to halt the initial Iraqi armored thrust.[79] After a brief initial hiatus, however, Iranian tacticians compensated for these deficiencies by avoiding large-scale battles wherever possible; instead they adopted guerrilla-style hit-and-run attacks aimed at Iraqi logistics. Iranian units began to harass Iraqi troops behind their fortified lines and hit targets in Iraq itself. The Iranian army used infantry extensively and armor sparingly (with some notable and disastrous exceptions) because of a lack of spare parts and because of its vulnerability to Iraqi antitank weapons.[80] Overall Iranian strategy, as it developed at the outset of the war, was to use delaying tactics to block any quick Iraqi victory in order to gain time to reorganize and mobilize vastly superior Iranian manpower.[81]

The slowness of the Iraqi advance facilitated the Iranians' ability to reorganize and make a defense. Iraqi planners had apparently thought that a sudden surprise attack spearheaded by an armored blitzkrieg would destroy what remained of Iranian military organization after the purges. To accomplish this, the Iraqis spread their attack over a broad front and crossed the border at four widely separated points. The follow-up advance was both slowly developed and relatively uncoordinated. The Iraqis held a major portion of their forces in reserve and committed them only much later to the fighting. Attacking Iraqi aircraft did not mount air strikes in sufficient numbers to put Iranian airfields out of commission. When Iraqi aircraft shifted to support of armored advances, their use was not coordinated with the ground units they were supporting.[82] The cautiousness of the Iraqi advance, of course, was due to other strategic considerations, but its effect was to nullify the advantage of initial surprise.[83]

Moreover, the expected uprising in Arab areas did not occur. In fact, advancing Iraqi forces found themselves opposed by the local Arab population in some areas.[84] Resistance apparently continued for some time, even though advancing Iraqi forces were extremely careful to move slowly enough to allow the inhabitants to move out of the area.[85]

Iraqi strategy was that of a limited war of attrition, and tactics were set in the context of an overarching political framework. This, in turn, was designated "Saddam's Qadisiyah" after the Arab/Muslim victory over Persian forces in A.D. 637. (The parallel with the Egyptian use of Islamic symbolism in 1973 is obvious.) This combined military/political plan called for a three-phase offensive: (1) a border crossing to occupy a number of border areas, including the oil complex in southern Iran; (2) an extension of Iraqi power down the Gulf to achieve control over the Shatt and regain the islands of Abu Musa and Greater and Lesser Tunbs (occupied by Iranian forces in 1971); and (3) the occupation of southern Iran and the subsequent creation of an Iraqi-dominated administration of that area.[86]

Tactically, two things were required to accomplish this: (1) a surprise attack that would allow Iraqi forces to envelop Iranian oil-producing centers rapidly, before any organized opposition could be mounted; and (2) a prolonged positional war, during which time Arab opposition to the Iranians in Khuzistan/Arabistan could be organized.[87] Beyond this, the subsequent conduct of the war was designed to exploit existing conflict patterns in Iran and the Gulf.

The Iraqi orchestration of the fighting had to be such that any Iraqi victory would not threaten the Arab coalition that initially supported Iraqi war aims. A fine policy line had to be followed. If the Iraqis succeeded in eliminating the Iranian threat to the Gulf, they could very well claim the leadership of a Gulf coalition. This in turn would clearly aid Iraqi ambitions in the Arab world. If, however, they were too successful militarily, they might find themselves opposed by their original supporters.[88] (In addition, of course, the war itself could be, and was, used as a rationale for moving aggressively against internal opponents: Shi'a, Kurdish, and communist.)

War, Linkage, and Spillover: The Regional Dynamics of a War of Attrition

Even though Iraqi strategy was designed to orchestrate some conflicts and to mitigate others, the eventual pattern of fighting led to unforeseen consequences. Iraqi planners felt that a war of attrition would work to their benefit—if it could be fought along certain lines. Unlike the war of attrition that the Egyptians had waged along the Suez Canal in 1973, Iraqi forces in Iran were potentially opposed by forces drawn from a much larger population base. Therefore, unlike the Egyptians who could count on numerical superiority, the Iraqis could not fight a war based strictly on numbers. They had to conduct the war in terms of logistics. In other words, the war had to be one of supply rather than manpower. Iraqi military strategy was designed to minimize the manpower cost of the war. Initially, Iraq committed only two of its thirteen divisions,[89] although more divisions subsequently became involved. Iraqi forces deliberately engaged in a lower level of fighting; aside from some initial advances to capture strategic positions, they remained dug in along defensive perimeters.[90] The idea was to force the Iranians to burn up their fuel and supplies in a series of counterattacks.[91]

Also implicit in Iraqi strategy was a concern for logistics. As a result of the wars with the Kurds, Iraqi planners had become extremely sensitive to the logistics dimension of any strategy requiring the employment of military forces. The problems and costs of moving and maintaining large forces in the north demonstrated the constraints that an inadequate logistical base could impose on any strategy. In fact, the Iraqis were keenly aware that the lack of a logistics capability could necessitate concessions on critical issues.

This "lesson" had been driven home several times. In a speech summarizing and explaining Iraqi concessions to Iranian territorial claims on the Shatt and other areas, concessions embodied in a "humiliating" treaty signed by both countries in 1975,[92] Saddam Hussein stated that the concessions resulted from an impossible logistics situation. According to Hussein, the Iraqis had initiated the negotiations that led to this treaty immediately upon the outbreak of the 1973 Arab-Israeli war because of a combination of factors: an increasingly threatening Kurdish insurgency, a potential threat of Iranian attack, a shortage of war matériel, and the necessity of detailing forces to aid in the defense of Damascus:

At that time, the Iraqi forces stood en masse on the eastern front as a precaution against an Iranian aggression on the national soil. In order to provide suitable circumstances for the Iraqi forces' participation in the battle against the Zionist enemy, the RCC [Revolutionary Command Council] issued a statement on 7 October 1973 in which it declared Iraq's readiness to settle the problems with Iran through peaceful means . . .

The issuance of this statement actually meant Iraq's readiness to look into Iran's demands in the Shatt al-'Arab. In 1975, President Boumedienne . . .

contacted Iraq and Iran and proposed direct negotiations between them in Algiers on the disputed matters. We agreed to this initiative.[93]

Even with the threat to the north temporarily eased, the Iraqi forces dispatched to Syria arrived in poor fighting condition. Much of the armor was forced to drive across the desert on its own treads, rather than being ferried by tanks transporters. The result, not surprisingly, was excessive engine and tread wear and, consequently, severe maintenance problems once the armor arrived in Syria.

This respite in the north was short-lived, and Iraqi forces once more engaged Kurdish insurgents in 1974. As noted above, the Iraqis were able to engage Kurdish insurgents with some success, but the costs were unexpectedly great. Iraqi commanders had to commit seven of the eight available divisions and 700 of the available 1,100 tanks. Casualties were high, and infantry morale dropped to the point where some units refused to fight in advance of their supporting armor. The result was a disastrous logistic and morale situation, which left Iraqi leaders no choice but to accede to Iranian demands:

> The Iraqi Army made great sacrifices in the battle which lasted for 12 months, between March 1974 and March 1975. In this battle, the Iraqi Army lost more than 16,000 casualties between martyred and wounded. The total losses of the people and the army amounted to more than 60,000 between martyred and wounded.
>
> . . . despite the high morale our army enjoyed, it was not possible to ignore the material and objective requisites of the battle. These requisites are sometimes important and decisive in determining political and military results . . .
>
> The situation became grave indeed when our basic ammunition and equipment were seriously depleted, particularly the decisive and most effective weapons. Ammunition for heavy artillery was almost exhausted. The air force had only three heavy bombs left . . .
>
> At the time, we concealed the fact of the grave shortage in our war materiel. We confined this information to an extremely limited scale within the leadership so that the enemy would not find out about this secret and continue their plots and aggressions, and so that our forces' morale would not wane and they would continue to fight bravely and honorably with other available weapons. However, this fact had an important impact on our political decision regarding the conflict between us and Iran.[94]

This gloomy assessment of the 1974–1975 fighting influenced Iraqi strategy in 1980. The cautious commitment of forces, along with a tactic of using as little infantry as possible and then keeping these units in defensive positions to minimize casualties, is traceable to the lessons of 1974–1976.

Logistics, Linkage, and Spillover

Even though the strategy was to hold a large percentage of ground forces in reserve,[95] the Iraqis were forced to commit an increasing number of troops to the Iranian front. To compensate for this manpower drain, they mobilized reserves and greatly expanded the Popular Army (some Popular Army units seem to have fought directly against Iranian forces).[96] As the war progressed, its logistics aspect assumed ever-greater importance and the combatants' need to secure adequate supplies triggered a process of coalition building in the region.

The dynamics of this coalition building, in turn, linked the war with still other conflicts and expanded its scope well beyond the site of the actual fighting. As the fighting took on the aspect of a prolonged and inconclusive war of attrition, the conflict, originally specific and defined, became increasingly diffuse and complex. Conflicts and actors not originally connected with the issues that led to the fighting became involved. Geographically and sociologically, the conflict spread through the Middle East in a concentric progression: as it moved away from the Iraq-Iran border, it also ramified throughout Middle Eastern social structure.

After deciding on war, the Iraqis turned their attention to the problem of securing alternative sources of arms. This problem, however, was more complex than just the acquisition of spare parts. Due to the variety of suppliers each side was forced to use, there was the problem of integrating arms from different weapons systems. Iraqi forces were equipped with Soviet arms, and the Soviets were their primary souce of resupply. In the first week or so of fighting, however, the Soviets cut off shipment of military supplies. Soviet ships bound for the Iraqi port of Basra turned around without unloading;[97] Soviet shipments were resumed only late in 1981. The Iraqis were, therefore, forced either to go to those countries whose forces were already equipped with Soviet weapons or to attempt to integrate Western arms with their existing Soviet weapons (which they did, in one instance, by arming Soviet fighters with French missiles).[98]

Perhaps in anticipation of problems with the Soviets, the Iraqis began to broaden their logistics base by negotiating with Western suppliers. In the summer of 1979, Iraq concluded arms-purchase agreements with both Spain and France.[99] During the war, the light and heavy military vehicles, light arms, and ammunition from Spain and the aircraft and electronics equipment from France were supplemented with troop carriers from Brazil, naval supplies from and naval training in Italy, and tank carriers and parts for British tanks (captured from the Iranians) from Great Britain.[100] All of these arms contracts called for payment in oil. When Iraqi oil was not available in emerged in response to the threat of Shi'a militancy in the Gulf: Saudi Arabia, Kuwait, and the UAE. These supplied the oil that the Iraqis used to barter for Western arms; later during the war, Saudi Arabia reportedly began shipping arms directly to the Iraqis.[102]As it became apparent that Iraqi forces would need large-scale resupply and that most of this had to be Soviet equipment, the coalition was expanded. Jordan was brought in during the first few days of the war. The Jordanian port of Aqaba was used as an alternative to Basra which was vulnerable to Iranian air strikes. In addition, Jordan supplied the vehicles for transporting military supplies across its territory.[103] The supplies themselves apparently came from Ethiopia and South Yemen, whose forces were Soviet-equipped.[104]

As Iraqi manpower needs mounted during the war, Jordanian involvement expanded. By early 1982, it had become obvious that additional manpower would be needed to offset Iranian numbers. (Iranians had adopted a strategy of "human wave" attacks to exploit their numerical superiority.)[105] In response, King Hussein announced the formation of a Yarmuk Brigade of 2,000 volunteers to aid the Iraqis.[106] Jordanian contingents were augmented by other Arab "volunteers." By February 1982 the commander of the Popular Army, Taha Ysain Ramadan, claimed that 10,000 volunteers had arrived from various countries, including Egypt, Jordan, the Sudan, Syria, Lebanon, and Tunisia, as well as from Muslim secessionist forces in Eritrea.[107] Of these, at least 7,000 were said to be Egyptians (former Egyptian army officers and men).[108] There were also reports that Moroccan leaders were considering sending regular troops to fight with the Iraqis.[109]

The Iranians had similar logistics problems. Iranian forces were equipped with U.S. weapons, and existing U.S. arms-transfer agreements had been suspended because of the hostage crisis.[110] Iranian resupply was brokered on one hand by the Syrians, who, in addition to supplying arms directly, trans-shipped Soviet equipment from Libya.[111] These arms were moved from Syrian ports across Turkey and into Iran. In return, Syria supplied arms to the Libyan-sponsored Islamic Legion operating in Chad, Niger, and reportedly the Sudan.[112] Syrian shipments were apparently supplemented by some direct Turkish arms sales. To the east, Pakistani arms flowed into Iran.[113] Libya reportedly paid for the Turkish and Pakistani arms.[114] In addition, Soviet equipment from North Korea was flown in through Pakistani airspace.[115]

The result again was an alteration of pre-existing alliance patterns; in this case by the creation of an Iranian-Syrian-Libyan alliance, with tacit Pakistani and Turkish cooperation. Syrian and Libyan help went beyond arms shipment. According to Iraqi sources, Iranian aircraft were allowed to use Syrian airfields, and the bodies of Syrian volunteers were discovered among Iranian dead.[116] There were also reports that Syrian pilots were flying some missions for the Iranian air force. By November 1980 there were unconfirmed reports of Libyan volunteers, both Libyan nationals and Libyan-trained Palestinians, operating in Khuzistan/Arabistan.[117] In May 1981 the Algerians allegedly started arms transfers to Iran. These shipments were said to include artillery shells, bazookas, mortars, antitank missiles, and spare parts, and they were sent to Iran by ship to Tartus in Syria and by air from Syria.[118] Unexpectedly, the Iranians received aid from two quite disparate sources. The Israelis began shipping arms, via Cyprus, in October;[119] and Soviet advisers began to move into Iran in November 1980.[120]

The resupply efforts of both Iraq and Iran generated a process of coalition and counter-coalition throughout the area—a process that led to a major shift in coalition patterns and ultimately to a repolarization of alliances in the area. In order to secure the support of members of the Arab Entente, the Iraqis were forced into a series of trade-offs. For example, Moroccan aid (both direct as an arms supplier and indirect as a broker for European suppliers) followed a shift in Iraqi policy on the Saharan conflict. From opposing Moroccan claims in the Sahara, the Iraqis switched in 1979 to a policy of supporting Morocco. Here, the Iraqis used what leverage they had with the Spanish and French governments to attempt to get both to back Moroccan aspirations.[121] In addition, the Iraqis supported Tunisia against the Libyans and allegedly even convinced the French to send arms to the Tunisians to aid them in combating Libyan-sponsored guerrilla attacks on Tunisian border posts.[122] This Iraqi shift triggered both a Libyan and an Algerian reaction.

The Libyans perceived Iraqi moves as the opening wedge in the creation of an alliance aimed at blocking Libyan moves in Africa. The Algerians also perceived this embryonic coalition as a threat and moved closer to the Libyans in response. The Saharan conflict was the focal point of these tensions prior to the war. Here, the Libyans and Algerians supported both the Polisario forces in the Western Sahara and the Mauritanians against the Moroccans and their allies. By 1981 tensions from the Iraq-Iran war both reflected and reinforced tensions flowing from the Saharan conflict. The Libyans claimed that Morocco had organized an unsuccessful attempt to overthrow Qaddhafi in March 1981; the Moroccans claimed that the Libyans were the chief supporters of Mauritania; and the Mauritanians, for their part, were providing Polisario forces with sanctuary.[123] The Libyans declared that any Moroccan attack on Mauritania would be considered an attack on Libya, and the Algerians began to ship arms to Mauritanian forces.[124]

Iraqi-Libyan-Algerian tensions were augmented by the Iraqi-Syrian-Jordanian hostilities. Syria and Jordan almost went to war in November/December 1980 and again in January/February 1981. Here the issue was Jordanian and Iraqi support for Muslim Brotherhood activities in Syria. The Jordanians permitted the Brotherhood to set up camps in the Ramtha area near the Syrian border. The Syrians moved troops to their side of the border, opposite these camps; the Jordanians reacted by interposing their own army units.[125]

These strategic alliances, based on logistics, were supplemented by an increasingly complex web of linkages: Syrian-Iraqi conflicts were extended in terms of a larger Shi'a-Sunni conflict. Syrian sponsorship of Shi'a opposition in Iraq paralleled Iraqi aid to the Muslim Brotherhood in Syria.[126] In addition, Palestinian groups were brought in. Iraqi-supported Palestinian hit teams operated in Syria; the Syrians replied with Palestinian hit teams of their own.[127] Kurdish tribesmen in Syria, Iraq, and Iran were aided by the various combatants.

An additional dimension was added by a secondary alliance of Marxists and Shi'ites in the Gulf. After the ICP's decimation by Iraqi security forces, it began to extend its organizational ties with other Arab Communists. It held a coordinating conference with fourteen other Arab communist parties in Prague in August 1981 in order to create a common strategy for overthrowing Hussein.[128] In turn, communist efforts were linked with Palestinian opposition to the Iraqis. Baghdad had already expelled two Palestinian groups, the Popular Democratic Front (PDF) and Popular Front for the Liberation of Palestine (PFLP), in late 1979 for their part in training Khomeini supporters. These groups began to forge organizational links with the ICP and its allies.[129] This alliance was extended into the Gulf by links with another coalition of Shi'as and Marxists that developed in early 1982.

In February 1982, a number of Gulf-based groups held a conference to coordinate their efforts to overthrow Gulf governments. Among those in attendance were communist parties from Iraq, Iran, North Yemen, Saudi Arabia, and Bahrain; Shi'a groups in the Peninsula (loosely coordinated as the National Democratic Forces in the Arabian Peninsula and Gulf); the Popular Front for the Liberation of Oman (PFLO); and the Islamic Republican party from Iran.[130]

This coalition was styled the Front for the Liberation of the Gulf, which, in turn, had ties with an as yet embryonic Islamic Liberation Army, a force jointly backed by Iran and Libya. In the wake of the Israeli invasion of Lebanon, this embryonic alliance took on an anti-Israeli caste with the addition of a Palestinian "revenge force." The revenge force was an amorphous group of younger Palestinians determined to avenge Israeli actions in Lebanon by launching a campaign of international terror. Initially, the revenge force was reported to be targeted at all moderate Arab governments and all U.S. interests in the Gulf and Europe. It portended a dramatic expansion of the Gulf conflict.[131]

Thus the Iraq-Iran conflict, which had originated on a narrow strategic level, extended to a multiplicity of levels during the course of the protracted fighting in Iran, as each side sought to acquire more and more allies and to attack the other side's coalition partners by aiding domestic opponents. As a consequence, the original scope of the war expanded into other areas as the linkage patterns tied in successively more combatants and auxiliaries. The Syria-Libya alliance, in effect, linked the Libyan conflicts with Chad, the Sudan, Egypt, Nigeria, Tunisia, and Morocco.[132] The Ethiopian–South Yemen connection tied in the Red Sea conflict.

All sides operated through a series of proxies in Lebanon: pro- and anti-Khomeini Shi'ites fought each other as extensions of Muslim-Christian coalitions; and the original Sunni-Shi'a conflict took on a Christian dimension as well because of Shi'a-Christian cooperation in Lebanon.[133] Moreover, the original Israeli-Iranian connection underwent a profound change with the Iranian decision to send "volunteers" to Syria to help the Syrians defend against a possible Israeli attack in the wake of the Israeli invasion of Lebanon in June 1982.[134] In addition, the Iranians co-opted the Palestinian issue into their call for the establishment of Islamic republics throughout the area by declaring that Jerusalem was the motherland of the Palestinians and Iran was willing to save this holy city from the Israeli occupation.[135] There were also unconfirmed reports that the Iranians invited the PLO to set up headquarters in "liberated Khuzistan" on the condition that the Palestinians support the Iranian strategy of overthrowing Sunni governments.[136]

Conclusion: Conflict, Strategy, and Polarization in the Middle East

Harold Lasswell once observed that there was a tendency toward polarization in an unstable conflict system.[137] Although this observation originally referred to European politics, it applies equally to the Middle East. Lasswell deduced this tendency from his theory that coalition behavior was an international extension of decision makers' personal needs for security. In the Middle East, this coalition-building behavior and the tendency toward polarization are an extension of strategies designed to cope with a multiplicity of conflicts. Unlike European conflicts, which are structured by stable boundaries that demarcate political units capable of controlling populations within them, Middle Eastern conflicts are diffused across political borders. In short, those definitions of sovereignty and jurisdiction that have been settled in Europe are still at issue in the Middle East. Middle Eastern conflicts are thus potentially unlimited in scope and undefined in nature.

From the overview presented above, it is apparent that the immediate factor claimed by the Iraqis as *casus belli*,[138] the conflict over control of the Shatt al-'Arab, was imbedded in a series of successively wider conflicts.[139] In turn, the sources of these conflicts were located in various aspects of Iraqi social structure: in the mosaic of communal groups crosscutting the Iraq-Iran border, in intracultural differences arising out of sectarianism, and in more straightforward factional patterns based on competing political ideologies. These different levels and types of conflicts were (and are) linked as the consequence of calculated organizational and political strategies on the part of those involved.

The Iraqi response to this pattern of conflicts was to escalate their conflict with Iran. The unexpectedly vigorous Iranian response, however, turned what was planned as a controlled war of attrition into a much more deadly conflict. As both opponents realized that the war itself would continue for some time, both sought an ever-wider circle of allies. The logistics dimension of the conflict became increasingly critical as the war was protracted over time and ever-larger amounts of war matériel (and critical manpower on the Iraqi side) were committed. This led both sides to search for arms suppliers, and the political trade-offs necessary to secure arms involved both sides in still other conflicts.

As the tide of battle began to shirt in Iran's favor beginning in the fall of 1982, the polarization process accelerated: Sunni Arab governments became increasingly apprehensive about the prospects of an Iranian victory and concomitant collapse of Iraq.[140] These regimes reacted by increasing their support for the embattled Iraqis. The July 1982 Iranian drive on Basra dramatized the Iranian threat to Gulf states' security to the point where the U.S. government felt compelled to assure these states that the United States would come to their aid. The increasing involvement of the United States added still another potential dimension—that of conflict between the superpowers.

In a parallel development, the Israeli drive on Beirut augmented the Arab-Israeli dimension, as the Palestinians and their supporters moved closer to the Iranian coalition. By later summer 1982, the coalitions formed in response to the Gulf fighting had begun to merge with older and more extensive coalitions formed around Arab-Israeli issues. Given the explicit Islamic dynamic of Iranian strategy, these more openly political coalitions became embedded in a more diffuse alignment growing out of issues generated by the Islamic revival.

It is this process of self-conscious linkage that provides the dynamic for Middle Eastern politics. Unlike European balance-of-power calculations, which are limited to the calculus of the relative power of states, Middle Eastern balance-of-power politics involved nonstate actors as well.[141] In the Middle East, coalitions based on shared strategic state interests are augmented by coalitions stretching out through layers of Middle Eastern social structure. State-based coalitions are thus reinforced by ethnic, sectarian, and class alliances. Conflicts are fought out on a number of different levels, and the combinations and permutations are almost infinitely variable. The complex dynamics of individual conflicts coalesce to create a tendency toward polarization throughout the region; coalitions and alliances are continually expanded by the addition of successively wider circles of states and organizations. Coalitions beginning at the level of states, therefore, tend to generate symbiotic coalitions of nonstate actors as well. Conversely, cross-national groups and organizations with their own conflict patterns tend to be co-opted into large combinations of opposed states.[142]

Notes

1. The concept of linkages requires some definition: a linkage is simply a relationship between one set of actors, or decision makers, and another set. It is any recurrent behavior pattern involving a reaction in one system to something that originated in another system (however defined). The actual connective sequence varies. It can be physical in the sense that personnel move back and forth between systems; it can be reactive in the sense that one actor reacts independently to actions and events elsewhere; or it can be emulative, whereby one set of actors imitates the behavior of others. (See James M. Rosenau, "Toward the Study of National-International Linkages," in James M. Rosenau, ed., *Linkage Politics: Essays on the Convergence of National and International Systems* [New York: Free Press, 1969], pp. 44–63.)

2. Claudia Wright, "Implications of the Iraq-Iran War," *Foreign Affairs* 59 (1980/81): 275–303.

3. Steven J. Rosen and Martin Indyk, "The Temptation to Preempt in a Fifth Arab-Israeli War," *Orbis* 20 (1976): 265–85.

4. Clinton F. Fink, "Some Conceptual Difficulties in the Theory of Social Conflict," *Journal of Conflict Resolution* 12 (1968): 412–60.

5. Robert A. LeVine, "Anthropology and the Study of Conflict: Introduction," *Journal of Conflict Resolution* 5 (1961): 3–15.

6. Wright, "Implications," pp. 275–76. See also *The Iraqi-Iranian Dispute: Facts v. Allegations* (Baghdad: Iraq, Ministry of Foreign Affairs, n.d.); and Salah al-Mukhtar, "The Iraqi Position," and Nasser Mobini, "The Iranian Position," in Ali Hillal Dessouki, ed., *The Iraq-Iran War: Issues of Conflict and Prospects for Settlement*, Policy Memorandum no. 40 (Princeton, N.J.: Princeton University, Center for International Studies, 1981), pp. 7–30.

7. Arms to Khomeini's followers were transiting Turkey, as were arms to Kurdish insurgents in both Iran and Iraq (*Arab Press Service*, 20 February 1979 and 25 April/12 May 1979).

8. As Wright ("Implications") points out, Iraqi decision makers were forced to contend with a policy environment characterized by extreme uncertainty. Not only can major governmental changes (such as the Shah's overthrow) suddenly appear in any of Iraq's neighbors, creating an entirely new and unforeseen set of strategic problems and threats, or both, but Iraqi targets are also within range of Israeli weaponry (as the

Israeli bombing of the nuclear reactor illustrates). Therefore, events in nonneighboring countries (such as the civil war in Lebanon) can trigger an escalation of threats to Iraq.

9. Saddam Hussein, "Address to the Nation," Baghdad Radio, 28 September 1980; reported in *Foreign Broadcast Information Service* (*FBIS*), *Middle East and Africa*, 29 September 1980.

10. Joe Stork, "Iraq: The War in the Gulf," *MERIP Reports*, no. 97 (June 1981): 12.

11. Ibid.

12. *Arab Press Service*, 10/17 October 1979.

13. Al-Da'wah was originally formed by Imam Mohammed Bakir Al-Sadr. The imam was executed by the Iraqis in 1980. Currently, al-Da'wah is headquartered in Tehran, although it receives Syrian support. Al-Da'wah spokesmen claimed responsibility for blowing up the Iraqi Embassy in Beirut on 15 December 1981.

14. The Syrians were also said to be supplying at least two Shi'a groups: al-Da'wah (see note 13) and the Iraqi Islamic Mujahidin, which also had Libyan connections (*Arab Press Service*, 20/27 May 1981).

15. See Stork, "Iraq," p. 7, for a summary.

16. The Pesh Merga, during that time, could mobilize between 50,000 and 60,000 fighting men (Richard Nyrop, ed., *Iraq: A Country Study* [Washington, D.C.: American University, 1979], pp. 226–27).

17. Ibid.

18. "Claim Kissinger Scuttled Kurd Revolt," *Chicago Sun Times*, 11 December 1975. The nucleus that remained in existence consisted of several groups: (1) the Kurdish Democratic Party (KDP), with about 3,000 Pesh Merga fighters still operating in the north, which is politically the "right wing" of the nationalism movement and receives aid from Iran, Israel, and Kurdish leaders living outside the Middle East; (2) the Unified Kurdish party (UKP), a coalition of smaller organizations, headquarters in Damascus, with some cells in northern Iraq and about 1,500 insurgents in the field, which operates in the border area of Syria, Turkey, and Iraq and has ties with leftist Kurdish groups in Turkey; and (3) the Patriotic Union of Kurdistan (PUK), which has especially close ties with the Syrian Communist party. The PUK has about 3,000 insurgents. It is nominally a Marxist party, but cooperates with al-Da'wah. (*Arab Press Service*, 20/27 May 1981.) The Kurdish national movement, however, is split between those Kurds following a tribal-based leadership and those following an urban intelligentsia. This split, which is reflected in the organizational heterogeneity of the movement, is crosscut by religious and class differences—differences accentuated by outside supporters: Iranian Kurds, for example, are divided into Shi'as and Sunnis; the Shi'as are dominated by a class of landlords and right-wing, middle-class families. These are pro-Khomeini because of religious reasons reinforced by Khomeini's support of them against the Shah's expropriation of their property during his land reform. The Sunni Kurdish community in Iran is somewhat larger and consists of a relatively poor peasantry. These are pro-Baghdad and receive Iraqi aid in fighting against the Iranian regime. Pro-Iraqi Kurds also receive arms from East European

states as well as from Turkish Kurds. These arms are in addition to weapons captured from imperial arms depots during the revolution. (*Arab Press Service*, 9/16 September 1979.) Iraqi Kurds are similarly divided: Sunni Kurds are predominantly landlords and merchants and are supported against the socialist Iraqi government by Iran and Israel. The PUK, which draws its support from these Kurds and is, oddly enough, a Marxist group, is aided by Syria and Libya. The Shi'a Iraqi Kurdish community consists mostly of peasants and poorer members of the middle class and is pro-Baghdad (in a reversal of what might normally be expected, since Iraqi Shi'a, in general, do not support the regime.)

19. Syria supplies a number of Kurdish groups: the Patriotic Union of Kurdistan of Jalal Talaban, which has links with al-Da'wah; the Unified Kurdish Socialist party; and the National Democratic party, which is headquartered in Damascus (see also *Arab Press Service*, 20/27 May 1981). For details on the Kurdish insurgency, see Ismel Sheriff Vanley, "Kurdistan in Iraq," in Gerard Chaliand, ed., *People Without a Country: The Kurds and Kurdistan* (London: Zed Press, 1978), pp. 153–210.

20. ICP-Libyan ties were reportedly brokered by the Syrians (*Arab Press Service*, 19 June 1978).

21. By 1974 the Iraqis had clear indications that the Syrians were also aiding Kurdish insurgents. The Syrians were supplying arms and allowing Kurdish forces to transit Syrian territory to stage attacks against Iraqi rear echelons (*an-Nahar Arab Report*, 3 March and 14 April 1975).

22. Syrian connections with various groups dated from the late 1960s: in 1969, Hafiz al-Asad, the then defense minister, allowed al-Sa'iqah units in Lebanon to train anti-Shah Khomeini followers. This connection was based on a more amorphous line between the 'Alawites of Syria and the Shi'ites of southern Iraq. In the middle 1960s, these Shi'a communities formed an intelligence network that passed information concerning the activities of SAVAK, the Iranian secret police, from Syrian 'Alawites to Iraqi Shi'a to Khomeini. (*Arab Press Service*, 20/27 May 1981.) (Al-Sa'iqah is the Syrian-sponsored and organized Palestinian organization, trained and supplied by the Syrian army. The 'Alawites are a schismatic Shi'a sect, geographically concentrated in northwestern Syria and southern Lebanon.)

23. For their part, the Syrians claimed that they had discovered an Iraqi spy ring that had penetrated Syrian Ba'th party cadres and also that Iraqi aid was being funneled to followers of Salah Jadid, whom Asad overthrew in 1970 (*an-Nahar Arab Report*, 14 April 1975). There was also a PFLP connection. The PFLP was itself an offshoot of the Arab Nationalist Movement (ANM), which, in turn, had contacts with Jadid's Ba'thist supporters.

24. *An-Nahar Arab Report*, 23 September 1974.

25. Ibid., 18 February 1974 and 8 July 1977.

26. *Arab Press Service*, 18/25 April 1979.

27. *An-Nahar Arab Report*, 24 February and 10 March 1975; and Stork, "Iraq," p. 11.

28. Some five Iraqi divisions were deployed opposite two to three Syrian divisions.

29. Including an assassination attempt on the Syrian prime minister (*an-Nahar Arab Report*, 2 December 1974; and *Arab Press Service,* 8 August 1978).

30. Hussein, "Address."

31. See also the excerpts from an interview with a senior Iraqi official in "Too Hot to Handle," *The Middle East*, November 1980, pp. 10–16, especially pp. 10–11.

32. *Arab Press Service*, 8/15 August 1979.

33. Some 600 Ba'th civilians and at least 120 officers were arrested, and a number of high-ranking officials were executed (ibid., 1/15 August 1979).

34. Hussein is said to have vowed that he would "never forgive" Asad for his "treachery and for having corrupted and caused the assassination of Saddam's best friends" (ibid., 5/14 September 1979).

35. The Iraqis had asked him to leave that August in an effort to ease tension with the Shah's government.

36. After Khomeini left Najaf, Shi'a populations rioted in Iran, and Shi'a gunmen attacked the Iraqi consulate at Khorramshahr (*Arab Press Service*, 17 October 1978).

37. As early as February 1979, the two countries concluded a security agreement to settle the problem of tribal movements across their mutual border.

38. In this case, leaders of both countries had agreed on the need to back the Shah against increasing Shi'a violence (*Arab Press Service*, 28 November 1978).

39. Khomeini had asked the Saudis for support in October 1978 and again in November. On both occasions, the Saudis had refused.

40. Many Gulf states have a high percentage of Shi'as: Kuwait—50 percent; UAE—20 percent; Oman—50 percent; Bahrain—75 percent; Qatar—40 percent (*Arab Press Service*, 13/20 February 1980).

41. Wright, "Implications."

42. *Arab Press Service*, 20 April/7 May 1981. See also George Lenczowski, "The Arc of Crisis: Its Central Sector," *Foreign Affairs* 57 (1978/79): 796–820; and J. C. Hurewitz, "The Middle East: A Year of Turmoil," *Foreign Affairs* 59 (1980/81): 540–77, for analyses of the impact of Iranian instability.

43. On the mosque takeover, see Jim Paul, "Insurrection at Mecca," *MERIP Reports*, no. 91 (October 1980): 3–4; and Adeed I. Dawisha, *"Saudi Arabia's Search for Security," Adelphi Papers*, no. 158 (Winter 1979–80): 250.

44. *Arab Press Service*, 28 November/5 December 1979.

45. Ibid.

46. Ibid., 27 August/3 September 1980.

47. Ibid., 20 April/7 May 1981.

48. See also ibid., 27 August/3 September 1980, for a summary of Hussein's comments.

49. Hussein, "Address."

50. Groups of Pesh Merga and ICP members attacked Iraqi installations in the north (Voice of Iraqi Kurdistan, 11 January 1981; in *FBIS*, 12 January 1981).

51. Apparently, this strategy worked. By January 1982, Arab sources reported that the Iraqi regime had been able to destroy the infrastructure of the Communists, Kurds, and pro-Syrian Ba'thists. Hussein personally ordered the release of imprisoned members of al-Da'wah in a gesture symbolizing his control over the country. (*Arab Press Service*, 13/20 January 1982.)

52. Wright, "Implications," p. 279.

53. Defense Minister 'Adnan Khayrallah, press conference of 25 September 1980; in *FBIS*, 26 September 1980.

54. *New York Times*, 27 September 1980.

55. For a summary, see James E. Dougherty and Robert L. Pfaltzgraff, Jr., *Contending Theories of International Relations* (New York: J. B. Lippincott, 1971), pp. 138–71 and 196–278.

56. In Western strategic thought, this would be termed "mini-max" thinking. See also the comments of the editors of the *Arab Press Service*, 3/10 December 1980, along the same lines. According to them, the Islamic dimension of the war outweighed strictly military considerations in determining tactics. Along these lines, Iraqi war propaganda had emphasized the "Persian" dimension of the conflict, portraying the war as an Arab versus Persian confrontation and calling on Arab Shi'ites to join their fellow Arabs in defeating the "racist" Persians and "magians." The Iranians, by contrast, have emphasized the Shi'ite aspect, describing Hussein as the "new Mu'awiya" or "new Yazid." (Ibid., 9 May 1981.) (Mu'awiya, the first Ummayad caliph, waged a successful civil war against 'Ali. Shi'as consider him responsible for 'Ali's death. Yazid, Mu'awiya's son, is responsible for the death of 'Ali's son, al-Husayn.)

57. In fact, it can be argued that Iraqi strategy is directly modeled on the 1973 Egyptian-Syrian campaign.

58. Sa'id Hamu, "War Preparation by the Motherland," *al-Jaysh al-Sh'ab* 8 (February 1981): 9–42; in *Joint Publications Research Service (JPRS)*, 21 September 1981, pp. 19–35.

59. The Popular Army was created in 1970 as a militia extension of regular Ba'th party organization. Popular Army units were organized in towns and villages to supplement Ba'th cadres. The new recruits were drawn from students (most schools and colleges were closed because of the war) and young women and men over the draft age, including merchants, teachers, and bureaucrats. Popular Army members served in areas where they lived and augmented regular police forces. Their main function was to patrol urban areas, enforce blackouts, and direct traffic. According to Arab sources, the Popular Army was indeed "popular," in contrast to the Iranian Revolutionary Guards, who were feared. (*Arab Press Service*, 4/12 November 1980; "The Popular Army and the Formula for Preparing an Armed Populace," *al-Jaysh al-Sh'ab* 9 [June 1981]: 74–77, in *JPRS*, 21 September 1981, pp. 13–17; and "The Popular Army: A Distinctive Experiment and Lofty Preparation in Defense of the Gains of the Revolution," *al-Jaysh al-Sh'ab* 9 [June 1981]: 49–54, in *JPRS*, 21 September 1981, pp. 4–9.

60. *Arab Press Service*, 18 October 1980.

61. Wright, "Implications," and Stork, "Iraq," p. 12.

62. Adeed I. Dawisha, "Iraq: The West's Opportunity," *Foreign Policy*, no. 41 (Winter 1980–81): 134–53.

63. *Arab Press Service*, 20/27 August 1980.

64. *New York Times*, 27 September 1980.

65. Abdul Rahman Siddiqi, "The Gulf War of Attrition," *Defence Journal* 6, no. 10 (1980): 1–10; and *New York Times*, 30 September 1980.

66. *Arab Press Service*, 29 October/5 November 1980.

67. Abolhasan Bani-Sadr, interview with Budapest television; in *FBIS*, 13 November 1980.

68. Bani-Sadr, interview by Eric Rouleau, *Le Monde*, 11 October 1980; in *FBIS*, 15 October 1980.

69. *New York Times*, 27 September 1980.

70. *Arab Press Service*, May 1981. There is some suggestion that Israeli intelligence was pushing the idea of a coup to topple Khomeini. See also the comments of Philip Tibenham, on the BBC program "Panorama," 1 February 1981; in *FBIS*, 4 February 1982. Tibenham interviewed both Ya-aqov Nimrodi, former head of the Mosad unit in Tehran, and David Kimche, head of the Israeli Foreign Ministry and former deputy director of Mosad. On the basis of these interviews, Tibenham claimed that Israeli intelligence viewed the Iraqi attack as a perfect opportunity to stage a coup and install military officers with whom the Israelis had acquired close connections during the Shah's years in power.

71. *Arab Press Service*, January 1981.

72. See also "The Fighting Men of the Autonomous Sector and the Battle of Saddam's Qadisiyah," *Al-Jaysh al-Sh'ab* 9 (June 1981): 204–16; in *JPRS*, 21 September 1981, pp. 30–33.

73. *Arab Press Service*, 1/8 October 1980.

74. Arab groups supported by the Iraqis included the Movement for the Liberation of Arabistan, the Popular Front for the Liberation of Ahvaz, and the Arab People's Organization. The Popular Front also received aid from Libya and the PFLP and ultimately split into two factions. (Ibid., 27 June/4 July and 18/25 April 1979.)

75. Ibid., 15/22 July 1981.

76. Siddiqi, "The Gulf War"; *New York Times*, 27 September 1980; and Stork, "Iraq," p. 12. Nevertheless, the purge of experienced senior officers was felt to the extent that the Iranian units were not well coordinated and their individual performance was poor during the early months of fighting. In particular, Iranian aircraft and their ground radar control were not effectively combined. The two missiles available to Iranian troops were not used in any comprehensive manner, and artillery fire was disorganized and off-target. Elsewhere, the lack of spare parts and other maintenance problems were evident after the first few days of fighting (*Washington Post*, 30 September 1980.)

77. Siddiqi, "The Gulf War"; and "Too Hot," pp. 10–13; on the organization and training of the Revolutionary Guards, see "Mullah–Revolutionary Guards Rift Crucial Threat to Regime," *Iran Press Service*, 29 October 1981, pp. 1–3; and Shahriar Rouhani, "Revolutionary Committees: The Essence of the Revolution," *Islamic Revolution* 1, no. 2 (May 1979): 30–31. The Guards (*Pasdar*) were the paramilitary arm of local revolutionary committees. These, in turn, were loosely organized under the nominal authority of a Revolutionary Council headed by Khomeini himself. The original function of the revolutionary committees was to replace the administrative apparatus destroyed by the revolution and the collapse of the Shah's government. The Guards themselves were also organized in a loose command structure whose commander was ultimately responsible to Khomeini. Their function was roughly equivalent to that of the SAVAK; that is, to achieve and maintain internal security and to hunt down opponents of the regime. The Guardsmen were paid a salary equivalent to that of junior-grade officers in the regular military. Because they were essentially an uncontrolled and unpredictable force, they were feared and hated by the populace, and their reputation prior to the war was akin to that of the SAVAK. They were, however, extremely zealous, and during the war this zeal was translated into their fighting ability. Originally, they were used in areas requiring hand-to-hand fighting: the defense of urban areas in the south and guerrilla-style operations in the central and northern areas. After the initial battles, the Iraqis began to avoid direct fighting with the Guards, preferring to use their superiority in artillery and mechanized warfare to deal with them at a distance, rather than exposing Iraqi infantry (largely recruited from Iraqi Shi'ites) to the Guards' Islamic zeal. The Iraqi strategy was to advance slowly behind a rolling artillery barrage and a lead wedge of armor, to stop and build a defensible line of bunkers and mine fields, and to engage Iranian troops with artillery, aircraft, and helicopter gunships. (*Arab Press Service*, 3/10 December 1980.)

78. The Iranians claimed they were outnumbered three to one on the ground and more than that in armor and aircraft.

79. Acting Chief of Staff Valiollah Fallahi admitted that Kurdish irregulars had tied down a critical number of Iranian troops and that this limited any response to the Iraqi attack (*Arab Press Service*, January 1981).

80. Ibid.

81. Bani-Sadr, interview with Budapest television; in *FBIS*, 13 November 1980.

82. Siddiqi, "The Gulf War."

83. After the Iraqi attack, Bani-Sadr claimed that Iranian intelligence had obtained the details of the invasion plan as well as a detailed account of "talks that took place in France among counter-revolutionaries, Iraqi representatives and US and Israeli military experts." This information was allegedly passed on to the Iranians by the KGB via Tudeh party representatives in Paris. The Iranians, initially, did not take this information seriously. (Eric Rouleau, "The War and the Struggle for the State," *MERIP Reports*, no. 98 [July/August 1981]: 3–8.)

84. Siddiqi, "The Gulf War."

85. According to Iraqi sources, the commanders of Iraqi forces investing Khorramshahr and Ahvaz both prolonged the siege to allow Arab inhabitants to leave and, wherever possible, avoided destruction of both lives and buildings (Hafiz Ibrahim Khayrallah, "Ziaul Haq Mission Ends with No Results: Al-Muhammarah Finally Falls and Siege of Ahvaz and Abadan Continues," *al-Sharz al-Awsat*, 2 October 1980, in *FBIS*, 3 October 1980; and "Too Hot," pp. 10–13).

86. Wright, "Implications"; Siddiq, "The Gulf War"; and *Arab Press Service*, 1/8 October 1981.

87. "Too Hot," pp. 10–13.

88. As the war developed and Iranian forces began to have some battlefield success in the later part of 1981, the difficulties in following this fine line surfaced. Gulf states that had initially offered assistance to Iraqi forces, by allowing Iraqi aircraft to be moved out of range of Iranian attacks and onto neighboring airfields, backed off, at least publicly, and assumed a very cautious political attitude toward the two combatants. (See William Quandt, "Reactions of the Gulf States," in Dessouki, *Issues of Conflict*, pp. 39–46.) Hussein found himself in an increasingly awkward position in that he was not able to show any overwhelming battlefield success (although Iraqi military strategy was such that no offensive thrusts were contemplated). His prestige suffered as a consequence, and his ability to lead a Gulf coalition diminished. Equally, the blunt Iranian refusal even to consider any mediation or other attempts to end the war gave the impression that the Iraqis, who had proposed numerous cease-fires, were increasingly anxious to get out of the war. This, according to Arab sources, further weakened Hussein's leverage in the Arab world. (*Arab Press Service*, January 1981.)

89. "Too Hot," pp. 10–13; and *Baltimore Sun*, 29 September 1980.

90. *Arab Press Service*, May 1981; Siddiqi, "The Gulf War"; and "Too Hot," pp. 10–13.

91. And again, there are parallels with the Egyptian strategy in 1973. One Arab analyst, Haytam al-Ayyubi ("Too Hot," pp. 10–13), points out that even when Iraqi forces were advancing, they did so with some care to minimize loss of both life and equipment.

92. Concessions involved the acceptance of the Iranian position on the Shatt al-'Arab. Heretofore, the Iraqis had maintained that the proper boundary between the two states was the eastern side of the Shatt, meaning that the entire waterway was under Iraqi sovereignty. The Iranians had argued that the correct boundary was determined by the thalweg, or midchannel, rule, meaning that sovereignty over the Shatt was shared by both states. A text of the treaty is available in *Arab World Weekly*, 28 June 1975, and the appendix to Dessouki, *Issues of Conflict*. The Iraqis abrogated this treaty on 18 September 1981, charging that Iranian violations were so flagrant that the treaty was already void.

93. Hussein, "Address."

94. Ibid.

95. Defense Minister 'Adnan Khayrallah, cited in *FBIS*, 25 September 1980; and "Too Hot," pp. 10–13. Regular ground forces numbered about 240,000 men.

96. Iraqi Popular Army forces were estimated to number 80,000 before the war; this number increased to over 300,000 during the fighting in 1981, with a total manpower goal of over 400,000 (*Arab Press Service*, April 1981). Some 60,000 Popular Army members were deployed on the front lines (*FBIS*, 8 February 1982).

97. *Washington Post*, 2 October 1980.

98. *Le Monde*, 28 March 1981; in *FBIS*, 3 April 1981.

99. *Arab Press Service*, 2/9 May 1979.

100. *Mid-East Intelligence Survey*, 16/28 February 1981; and *Arab Press Service*, April 1981. Like the Israelis in 1967 and 1973, the Iraqis made use of captured Iranian equipment, either intact or cannibalized for parts. Among the equipment captured were British Chieftain and U.S. M-60 tanks, TOW antitank missiles, and 155 mm guns.

101. Saddam Hussein, interview in *al-Hawadith*, 17 April 1981; in *FBIS*, 23 April 1981.

102. According to Israeli sources, the Saudis were giving the Iraqis U.S.-made field guns (*Arab Press Service*, 30 September/7 October 1981).

103. *Washington Star*, 8 October 1980. After the Israeli attack on the Iraqi nuclear reactor in June 1981, Jordanian-Iraqi military cooperation was expanded. The Jordanians agreed to provide Iraq with extended air defense coverage to prevent further such attacks. Reportedly, the Iraqis also asked the Saudis to provide additional radar coverage to the south. (*Arab Press Service*, 17/24 June 1981.)

104. *New York Times*, 8 October 1980.

105. Kamal Hasal Bukhayt, "Iraqi Vigilance Aborts Blind 'Attack of Millions,'" *al-Watan al-'Arabi*, 18/24 December 1981, pp. 24–25.

106. *Arab Press Service*, 17/24 February 1982.

107. Ibid.

108. *An-Nahar Arab Report*, 3 February 1981. The Egyptians have denied this report.

109. *Arab News*, 5 February 1982.

110. Some U.S. shipments apparently did arrive in Iran. Consignments of arms worth about $480 million, which had already been set for delivery, were shipped in 1981. In September 1981, the Iranians contacted the United States through Algeria and attempted to get replacement parts for the Iranian air force. Part of the desperation behind this effort was due to difficulties with other sources of U.S. arms, specifically with the Israelis and Taiwanese. Both of these suppliers had adopted a cash-and-carry policy, and the Iranians were having difficulty raising the funds. In addition to a straight arms deal, the Iranians wanted the U.S. government to release some $2 billion worth of Iranian assets frozen in U.S. banks and tied up by lawsuits. The Iranians were said to have made settlement offers totaling $600 million of these claims. (*Sunday London Times*, 27 December 1981.)

111. *New York Times*, 30 September 1980. Libya reportedly cut off arms supplies to Khomeini in September 1981 (*Iran Press Service*, 10 September 1981). The Syrian

connection antedated the war by some time. Al-Saʻiqah had been training Khomeini followers at its base in Lebanon for some time, and Syrian aid apparently found its way to an anti-Iraqi Shiʻa group, al-Amal. (*Arab Press Service*, 23/30 April 1980.)

112. Israeli Radio, 21 October 1981; in *FBIS*, 22 October 1981.

113. *New York Times*, 30 September 1980.

114. The Libyans reportedly offered Turkey double the going price for F-4s and F-5s, the mainstay of the Iranian air force (*Arab Press Service*, 19/26 November 1980).

115. Ibid.

116. Baghdad Radio, 12 October 1980 and 2 September 1981; in *FBIS*, 13 October 1980 and 3 September 1981.

117. *Arab Press Service*, 5/12 November 1980.

118. Ibid., May 1981. The Algerians have denied these reports.

119. Ibid., 5/12 August 1981.

120. Ibid., 27 January/3 February 1982.

121. Ibid., 5/12 March 1980.

122. Ibid.

123. Ibid., 1/8 April 1981.

124. Ibid.

125. Ibid., 10/17 December 1980.

126. Ibid., 30 April/7 May 1980 and 5/12 August 1981.

127. A coalition of groups hostile to the Iraqi regime, collectively known as the National Progressive and Democratic Front in Iraq, was formed in December 1981. Its headquarters was reported to be in Damascus. It claimed to have training bases in a number of countries, with operating bases in Iraq itself. Syria was its main source of arms, but other members of the Steadfastness and Confrontation Front provided some backing. The Iranians also apparently supplied aid. (*Arab Press Service*, 10/17 December 1980.)

128. Voice of Lebanon, Beirut, 20 August 1981.

129. *Arab Press Service*,, 1/8 April 1981.

130. Ibid., 3/10 February 1982. A number of other groups were apparently connected with this congress, either directly or indirectly, as a result of Shiʻa ties. A cluster of Islamic liberation movements were sponsored by the Iranians and linked to the congress via Iranian connections: the Islamic Liberation Movement of Iraq, the Islamic Alliance for the Liberation of Afghanistan, the Moroccan National Revolutionary Front, the Islamic Revolutionary Organization of the Arabian Peninsula, the Islamic Front for the Liberation of Bahrain, and the Islamic Organization for the Liberation of Oman. (See *FBIS*, 20 November 1981, for the names of these organizations; and *Arab Press Service*, 27 January 1982, for details on some of these groups.)

131. *Arab Press Service*, 11/18 August 1982.

132. Ibid., 18/25 February 1981.

133. Ibid.

134. Ibid., 3 October 1978; and 6/13 May 1981.

135. Ibid., 21/28 July 1982.

136. Ibid., 14/21 July 1982.

137. H. D. Lasswell, *World Politics and Personal Insecurity* (Glencoe, Ill.: Free Press, 1950), pp. 54ff.

138. See also *The Iraqi-Iran Dispute: Facts v. Allegations* (Baghdad, Iraq, Ministry of Foreign Affairs, n.d.).

139. Ibid.

140. See also David Hirst, "The Gulf Power Shift: The Consequences of an Iranian Defeat of Iraq," *Manchester Guardian*, 16/19 April 1982.

141. Even in Europe, there are groups—Muslims in the Soviet Union, Croats in Yugoslavia—whose loyalty to the central state is open to question and who might, in the event of conflict, be exploitable by a foreign state. In general, however, the state is the focus of most citizens' political loyalties, and the types of cross-national linkages discussed in this paper do not exist.

142. See also Richard N. Rosecranz, *Action and Reaction in World Politics: International Systems in Perspective* (Boston: Little, Brown & Co., 1963).

5 | The Gulf Cooperation Council

John Duke Anthony

This essay focuses on six of the Gulf states: Saudi Arabia, Kuwait, Bahrain, Qatar, the United Arab Emirates (UAE), and Oman. Now is a propitious time to consider the status and roles of these countries. The reason should be underscored, for it is by no means obvious to many Westerners: a major change in the relations of each of these states both to the other five and, in the context of the six as a group, to the world at large. In essence, the early 1980s mark the end of one of the most productive decades in their history and the beginning of an unprecedented one.

It is important to recall that, in 1971, after being responsible for their defense and foreign relations for more than a century, Great Britain abrogated its long-standing special treaty relationships with three of these states— Bahrain, Qatar, and the seven emirates that now constitute the UAE. The period since then has seen an immense transformation for the people who live and work in the Gulf. As they pursue their interests, concerns, and requirements in the 1980s, increasingly through their own institutions, this transformation is expected to continue.

The GCC's Establishment

One of the most significant events since 1971 was the establishment of the Gulf Cooperation Council (GCC). Despite the presence of representatives from most of the world at the Council's inauguration on 25 May 1981 in Abu Dhabi, U.S. media gave the event, then and subsequently, scant notice.

The Council, formally proclaimed shortly after the Organization of the Islamic Conference (OIC) Summit in Saudi Arabia in January 1981, had a busy first year. Since then, nine meetings of the Council's foreign ministers and four meetings of all six heads of state have produced important results. Not the least were the early commissioning of working papers by Kuwait on economic issues and by Oman on regional security. These papers were considered at the summit in Abu Dhabi and, in more elaborated form, at the Ministerial Council's meeting of 31 August–1 September 1981 in Ta'if, Saudi Arabia. The Council also reached unanimous agreement at the Abu Dhabi summit on the choice of a secretary general: Kuwait's Abdallah Bishara, who had represented his country with distinction at the United Nations.

Bishara's selection was considered a political master stroke, enhancing prospects for greater Kuwaiti moderation on foreign policy matters, and encouraged greater involvement of the Kuwaitis, with their considerable expertise, in GCC activities. The Ta'if meeting resulted in two additional accomplishments that strengthened the Riyadh-based Secretariat. Two deputy secretaries general were chosen: Abdallah al-Ghuwayz from Saudi Arabia, for economic affairs, and Salim Subhi from Oman, for political affairs.

Underscoring the importance of these developments in regional security issues was another milestone, a meeting at Riyadh in September 1981 of the chiefs of staff of the GCC states' armed forces. This meeting, a major breakthrough in intraregional military cooperation, ended with the six force commanders agreeing with the Omani working paper on regional security and a separate Saudi paper on related issues. By the fourth heads of state summit in November 1983 at Doha, Qatar, there had been four such meetings. They represented events of great importance for Western interests and involvement by these states. Yet the number of influential Americans who are aware of the Council's existence is minuscule.

Organization, Structure, Expectations

Compared with other regional institutions, the GCC's structure is relatively simple. The principal policymaking body is the Supreme Council, comprising the six heads of state, with a presidency that rotates in alphabetical order by country. Enjoined by the GCC charter to convene every six months, the Supreme Council met in Abu Dhabi in May 1981, in Riyadh during November of that same year, in Bahrain in November 1982, and in Doha, Qatar, in November 1983. Additional extraordinary meetings may be called as necessary, and any member may call a Ministerial Council meeting, so long as this is seconded, as in May 1982, when the ministers met to deliberate the deteriorating status of the Iraq-Iran war.

The Supreme Council is responsible for higher policies and the basic mode of operations and for discussing recommendations, rules, and regulations submitted for approval by the Ministerial Council and the Secretariat. It also is responsible for appointing members to a GCC Conciliation Commission. This little noticed, potentially important, arm of the GCC has yet to be created. Meanwhile, its mandate to help resolve existing or potential disputes among members has been carried out by Kuwait and the UAE on behalf of the GCC. One of their impressive achievements has been to end amicably the long-standing disputes between Oman and the People's Democratic Republic of Yemen.

Reporting to the Supreme Council is the Ministerial Council, consisting of the six foreign ministers, which meets bimonthly, with provisions for convening extraordinary meetings on the vote of two or more members. By the fourth GCC heads of state summit, in November 1983, there had been nine meetings of the Ministerial Council.

Considering the GCC's organization and structure, many observers have mistaken it for yet another experiment in Arab "unity." It is clear that conceptually, politically, and organizationally the GCC is not working toward unity, merger, or other forms of structural integration. The words "union," "unity," "fusion," or similar sentiments have seldom been heard in most of the discussions, debates, and decisions to date. Rather, on matters of common concern, the words and concepts most frequently voiced have been "standardization," "harmonization," "collaboration," "coordination," and, especially, "cooperation"—as in the name the members chose for the Council. The six are pursuing these concepts through a number of themes that bestow upon the GCC less an ideological base than a broadly similar set of interests and concerns.

Central Concerns and Themes

Security

Despite the initial and ongoing emphasis on economic, social, informational, and educational cooperation envisioned and enshrined in the earliest GCC communiqués—and in the charter itself—security concerns quickly occupied those who set the Council's priorities. With the Iraq-Iran war raging barely twenty minutes away from their borders, the need to find a credible and effective means to deal with the problems of security was, of course, among the most compelling reasons for establishing the GCC. Whatever regionwide concerns competed for the attention of the heads of state, the final arbiters of Council policies and actions, security surpassed all others in their minds.

The danger of inaction on the security issue became increasingly clear and ominous as the war between Iraq and Iran continued. Many GCC members believed that the longer the time between the end of that conflict and the date the six heads of state could agree to cooperate on defense and security matters, the more likely Iraq or Iran, or both, would seek to influence the Council's deliberations. Those states' armed forces have recently been tested in battle and are twice the size of the combined armies of all GCC states, which underscores the sense of tension and vulnerability in the Gulf.

GCC meetings on security issues served dual objectives. First, before others could intervene or provide a distraction, they helped nail down a vital plank in the cooperative mechanism being built. Second, they moved the consensus among the group on security issues from the level of conviction to specific undertakings and commitments. The most significant achievement was the three-week joint military exercise on UAE soil in October 1983 involving a combined force of 6,500 troops from the six states' armies.

Economic and Social Functionalism

Differing versions of functionalism appeal to the administrative personnel on whose labors the day-to-day work of the Council's affairs depend. There are increasing references to notions such as "common units" (for example, departments in the six states responsible for civil aviation matters dealing with common problems such as fare increases, routing, and airport locations in a communal milieu.)

The more ambitious in the Council, who would like to negotiate agreements using this approach, frequently refer to the European Economic Community (EEC) and, to a lesser extent, the Association of Southeast Asian Nations (ASEAN) as examples toward which the Council should move. Yet, whether the GCC should think in EEC terms remains highly debatable to some; others, however, support the view that functionalists should be encouraged to determine whether anything of significance might be achieved this way.

The success of comparable groupings suggests that their tangible achievements over time have often been closely identified with the functionalists. The GCC functionalists believe the evidence indicates that the successes of other cooperation-oriented institutions have been the fruit of the labors of individuals who, less by personality than by similar training, outlook, and responsibility, have made the institution work on a day-to-day basis, operated with this approach.

A budding consensus among the GCC's technically oriented development planners and economists is that the GCC should first achieve gradual economic cooperation. If successful, this should enhance the prospects of forging a measure of collective security. However, GCC critics contend that using the

EEC as a model is unrealistic and distorted since the GCC states have not been devastated by war, have not been prodded toward concerted economic planning, and are unlikely to have a NATO providing a security umbrella while its members work out their economic relationships.

Culturally and ideologically, the most comprehensive of the value systems permeating the GCC countries is clearly *Islam*. Islam provides the broadest umbrella for the largest number of participants and permits the greatest flexibility in criteria for admitting additional full or associate members. It is also the easiest reference point for the public to encourage and endorse their self-identity and has helped in maintaining relations with both Iran and Iraq.

An additional consideration bearing on the Council's Islamic image is the status and role of Pakistan. The Islamic image has facilitated the agreements and understandings of a military and security nature between Pakistan and individual Council members. Moreover, apart from Iraq, Iran, and Pakistan, the Islamic face of the Council has helped promote organizational and political cooperation between GCC and Muslim countries and organizations further afield—such as the 42-member OIC.

In contrast to Islam, *Arabism* has been less emphasized in the Council's deliberations and communiqués. When stressed, it has usually reflected the GCC's manifest need to demonstrate—to other League of Arab States members—that the Council confirms the Arab character of the six. In drafting statements on this issue, however, the GCC has chosen not to offend unwittingly either the perceptions and sensitivities of Iran, non-Arab minorities elsewhere in the Gulf, other OIC members, or the regionalist pretensions to pan-Arab leadership espoused by Iraq.

The concept of regionalism, like those of Islam and Arabism, has several dimensions in the Council. The geographical notion most often associated with the term has obvious validity, yet this dimension has been largely de-emphasized. The area in which the Council has established itself as a cooperative body—the north Arabian Peninsula littoral—has seldom been referred to as a region in its own right. Additionally, the region in which the six are located—the Gulf—is not fully represented in the GCC owing to the absence of Iran and Iraq. Some would argue that another factor compounding matters at the perceptual level is that the Arabian Peninsula in which the six are located is not fully represented due to the absence of North and South Yemen. GCC planners were aware from the outset that attributing any unique geographic characteristics to the Council would probably heighten the isolationist concerns and adversarial attitudes of Iraq, Iran, and the two Yemens.

A further geopolitical consideration is that highlighting the regional dimension of the Council's nature and orientation would obscure the more significant commonalities among its members. These stem as much from the similarities in their history, culture, economy, and forms of rule as from geographic considerations, which, by comparison, are less significant. By emphasizing the similarity of governmental institutions and political systems among the six, the Council's members have implicitly and subtly made a case for limiting GCC membership to themselves, at least for the time being.

Patterns of Cooperation

Especially noteworthy in the area of cooperation is that many of the functions it has rationalized were hardly foreign to the six. This has been difficult for many observers, particularly Americans, to grasp. Cooperation in the GCC, in their view, is taking place among states dismissed not long ago as unlikely to contribute to the orderly development of the region.

What many have overlooked, however, is that Bahrain, Qatar, and the UAE, fully sovereign actors in regional and world affairs, are more than ten years old. The other three are much older. Saudi Arabia, clearly the most important of the six, has passed the half-century mark as an independent country, Kuwait has been independent for more than two decades, and Oman, in some ways, seems older than time.

Despite a general international impression, the GCC did not emerge from a vacuum. The Council's birth was the logical culmination of a decade-long movement to impose a degree of order on the dozens of bilateral and multi-lateral agreements and understandings among these states.

In scope, their agreements and understandings dealt with everything from civil aviation to the standardization of educational curricula, the exchange of information, proposals for a common understanding, and a customs union; the establishment of joint economic ventures, harmonization of development programs, and collective security agreements among the members. In short, abundant evidence of a decade-long tradition of regional cooperation among the six highlights a pattern among these states of less deference to some of their senior Arab sisters and more reflection on their own perceived interests. Historically, this indicates a significant development in the intraregional relationships of the six.

An additional area of GCC concern is the age-old question of territorial boundaries, high on the Council's agenda. The Iraq-Iran war has provided compelling evidence that contested border claims can create tension in inter-state relations. The 1960s, 1970s, and 1980s reveal a significant record by the six in settling their border disputes. Those between Kuwait and Saudi Arabia (onshore), between Saudi Arabia and Qatar, between Qatar and the UAE, and between the UAE and Oman are no longer at issue. To be sure, several disputes remain: the Bahrain-Qatar dispute over the Hawar Islands, the lack of agreement between Saudi Arabia and Kuwait over the location of their common maritime frontier, and the undemarcated boundary between Oman and Saudi Arabia. The point to be underscored, however, is that GCC leaders have accorded this problem a high priority.

Stability

Another major GCC concern is stability. Ten years ago it was questionable whether some of the GCC states could survive half a decade as independent states.

Viewed from the Western world, there was perhaps valid cause for concern. The reasons have a familiar ring. They included the small size of several of the states' native populations, the large foreign labor force, the seemingly frenetic pace of economic and social development, immense strains from beyond their borders, and their limited expertise in dealing with the envy their energy and wealth arouses among less well endowed countries.

Fears of instability in this area has been a constant theme of the outside world's concerns. Yet, despite the fears voiced by U.S. senators during the acrimonious debate over the sale of Airborne Warning and Control Systems (AWACS) planes to Saudi Arabia, an accurate perception would be different. The Western stereotypes about instability in the GCC area have been more misleading than insightful or informative.

The reference is to statements passing for conventional wisdom about the Gulf by high-ranking Western officials who postulated that the GCC region is "one of the most turbulent and politically unstable areas in the world." Yet analyses reveal such assertions to be only half-truths about the Gulf.

If the focus is on interstate relations outside the GCC area (for example, among the eastern Mediterranean or North African countries, or adjacent to the GCC in Iran and South Yemen and their neighbors), there has been considerable turbulence and instability. But the objective analyst might acknowledge that relations *between* states constitute only half, and perhaps the least significant half, of elements of stability in a region.

The other half of regional stability concerns what occurs *inside* the states. At the governmental level, it is within the states that most treaties are negotiated. It is within these states that arms agreements, diplomatic understandings, and other undertakings are reached. It is within the states that a broad range of economic, commercial, financial, investment, and development transactions occur every day. These states are among the most politically stable societies not only in the Middle East but also in the category of developing countries.

An often heard question is "Stable? By what standards?" GCC spokesmen reply in terms of the following criteria: by the small number of protest movements, demonstrations, and riots in the GCC states during the decade; by the paucity of clandestine cells and revolutionary printing presses uncovered or believed to exist; by the low level of crime in these societies and by the absence of successful—or even attempted—coups d'etat; by the near absence of citizen unemployment; and by the limited alienation among the politically aware that would otherwise be ubiquitous if human aspirations or societal opportunities were seriously limited or stifled.

In underscoring additional common sources of strength, GCC spokesmen emphasize that while each state has its own peculiar mix of social and political problems, as a group they share similar attributes contributing to continued political stability. Among the similarities are that each of the six benefits from a good relationship with the West and acknowledges that the United States exercises a subtle great power role by checking Soviet military intervention in the area. All six GCC regimes have impressive records of using their oil wealth to improve the economic and social lot of their citizens. Bahrain and Oman, the two least affluent GCC members, have benefited substantially from the financial aid programs of the other four. All six governments have demonstrated a practical focus on building a decent environment, and the appeal of radical and revolutionary doctrines, from neighboring and distant Arab countries, has diminished greatly. Using somewhat similar variables, Edward Azar of the University of Maryland examined a broad range of countries. An important conclusion of his study was that Saudi Arabia, headquarters for the GCC Secretariat and the GCC state most frequently characterized by Western critics since the 1950s as "unstable," has been one of the world's most "stable" countries. The criteria for stability were the consistency and predictability of Saudi policies, important determinants for those who are charged with making political judgments, investment decisions, and strategic assessments.

Security

Closely related to stability, of course, is security. No GCC head of state needs to be reminded of its controversiality or explosiveness. Each of the four summits, virtually all the nine meetings of the GCC Ministerial Council, and all four meetings of the armed forces chiefs of staff have discussed security questions.

The concern with security issues is a direct outgrowth of GCC members' perceptions of threats to their societies. From the numerous meetings of the Council evolved a consensus among the six that there are four challenges to their external security: Iran, Israel, the Soviet Union, and the United States.

Most of the six agree that the Soviet Union represents the greatest long-term danger to their security. However, they view the long term as but the sum of short terms. And in considering the short term, the two most immediate and persistent threats to their security have been the spillover effects of the Iraq-Iran war and, for a longer period, an expansionist and intransigent Israel.

They increasingly relate the Israeli threat to their fourth security concern—the United States.

The perceived relationship between the Israeli and the U.S. threats, long in the minds of Gulf citizens, took on added substance when in 1981 Israel bombed Beirut and violated Saudi Arabia's and Jordan's airspace en route to bombing a nuclear reactor in Iraq. Israeli overflights of Saudi Arabia's air base at Tobuk underscored persuasively the weakness of the GCC air surveillance and defense capabilities.

Within GCC circles, approval of the AWACS sale was not just a matter of great importance for the future course of U.S.-Saudi relations. And, it was not just important to the Saudi Arabian government and its constituents, who were led by the United States to believe that the word of two presidents could be trusted. There was a third dimension: the linkage of that sale, and possible future ones, to GCC regional security concerns.

Despite a concerted campaign of misinformation by opponents, all the GCC countries strongly favored approval of the AWACS sale. Had it not passed, there is little doubt that the views of these five additional states about forging closer security ties with the United States would have taken a turn for the worse.

The Israeli raids served to blur even further what, for many GCC states, was an already blurred distinction between the policies and actions of the United States and those of Israel. And, as if those events were not enough to call into question the credibility of U.S. commitments in the Gulf, another had that effect: the Israeli invasion of Lebanon.

American analysts seeking the source of GCC concern over the relationship between the United States and Israel should focus less on their own concerns and more on the Gulf Arabs' concerns. Coming to terms with the latter entails viewing security, strategy, and stability in the Middle East in ways that often differ from the Western viewpoint.

Many of the Arab leaders recognize that the United States has strategic interests in the Persian Gulf and that each Gulf state has something of strategic value to offer. None would challenge the view that in terms of the United States' national security interests, some GCC and other Middle Eastern countries have valuable raw materials or excellent harbors, and two (Saudi Arabia and Oman) have vast airspace. GCC spokesmen acknowledge that some regional countries are important in terms of technology, others have sizable populations, and some offer lucrative markets.

Still, GCC officials argue that some countries are of considerably less strategic value than others. The example they cite most frequently with respect to the GCC is Israel. They are among the first to acknowledge that Israel may offer certain strategic values to the United States. But there is hardly a GCC spokesman who does not insist that U.S. policy on this matter is seriously misguided. Indeed, the United States, in the GCC's view, has linked itself not with a strategic asset but with a strategic liability.

Americans persistently fail to see the logic and rationale of such views. GCC spokesmen have often responded by asking the skeptical to consider what the United States has stated to be among its primary interests in the area. Citing a host of U.S. officials, they tend to emphasize (1) diminishing the opportunities for the Soviet Union to increase and expand its interests and involvement in the area; (2) ending the Arab-Israeli conflict; (3) bringing to a just and lasting settlement the festering Palestinian problem; (4) creating an atmosphere conducive to cooperation rather than confrontation in energy affairs—particularly petroleum pricing and levels of production; and (5) enhancing the prospects for regional security cooperation. There is hardly one of these interests with which the six would take issue in terms of legitimacy. Although the GCC states often formulate them differently, these are their interests too.

For the United States to pursue such interests in a credible and effective manner, GCC leaders believe that Washington must work closely with countries in which its most vital interests lie. What they hear, however, is that a special strategic relationship is to be forged with Israel. Their consternation is compounded by Israel's status as a single, non-Arab, non-Islamic country that happens to be situated not on the Gulf but rather on the Mediterranean.

This is only part of the concern of many GCC spokesmen over the rationale behind the U.S. intention to elevate its already special relationship with Israel to a level of strategic partnership. As GCC officials never tire of emphasizing to Westerners, acknowledging that many U.S. interests in their part of the world are legitimate is one thing. However, living and working in the area and believing that international misunderstanding and mistakes are often causes of danger, they stress their continuing concern about the matter and the means by which the United States pursues its interests.

Such spokesmen profess puzzlement at the way the United States attempts to maintain and enhance its Middle East objectives. In their view, no country could realistically hope to pursue its interests in a given region through the device of a single institution, government, or head of state. Rather, regional realities require that the United States, no less than any other foreign power, work with and through both the individual Middle Eastern states and such regional organizations to which they belong.

GCC leaders acknowledge that the United States has relations with some two dozen Middle Eastern countries—nearly twenty Arab states, plus non-Arab Cyprus, Iran, Israel, Pakistan, and Turkey. GCC strategists wonder whether Americans have considered the regional picture as it looks to GCC citizens.

As Gulf strategic analysts view the region, no other country among the 24 states in this area has done more than Israel to—

1. Cause regional instability.
2. Seize real estate.
3. Remain diplomatically isolated, regionally and globally.
4. Guarantee bankruptcy should foreign aid be withdrawn.
5. Flout the U.S. Arms Export Control Act.

From the foregoing, GCC leaders have concluded that, of the 24 states in the area, Israel is the least suitable country for facilitating the needs and interests of the United States. The conclusion is a harsh and devastating indictment of U.S. foreign policy pertaining to U.S. interests and attitudes vis-à-vis the Gulf. Yet the tone is as much one of sadness and dismay as it is of anger and alienation. It is the more regrettable since it comes from a bloc of states whose regional and international interests are broadly comparable to those of the United States.

6 | U.S. Policy and Gulf Security

Charles G. MacDonald

The revolution in Iran and the Soviet invasion of Afghanistan sent shock waves throughout the Gulf and around the world. The Arab Gulf states faced the reality of new revolutionary forces that had not only reached the Gulf, but had overthrown the heretofore most powerful leader in the region. The "island of stability" that the Shah's Iran appeared to be, crumbled when the Shah's authority gave way to the fundamentalist Islamic forces that co-opted the energies of Iranian nationalism and swept away the U.S. policy of relying on the Shah to ensure stability in the region. Following the seizure of American hostages in Iran, the Soviet invasion of Afghanistan in December 1979 brought home the reality of a Soviet threat to Iran and to the Gulf. The United States and other Western industrial powers that had become dependent on the energy resources of the Gulf, at least in the near term, faced a possible cutoff of Gulf oil. Such a cutoff could bring economic disaster to the West and fragment the Western alliance, as Western states scrambled for limited energy resources.

The growing influence of Islamic militancy, with its anti-imperialist/anti-U.S. rhetoric, together with the specter of a Soviet military advance, created a new sense of urgency in Washington's search for an effective policy to protect vital U.S. interests in the Gulf. At the same time, Arab Gulf states, watching the excesses of the Iranian Revolution and fearing its possible spread, came to re-evaluate their own search for security—a security that is by no means identical to that envisioned by the United States. In fact, they perceive the

United States as a potential threat in some situations, though a necessary partner in others.

Presently, as the full impact of the Airborne Warning and Control Systems (AWACS)/F-15 enhancement sale to Saudi Arabia is yet to be realized, it is apparent that the United States is moving to project a strong commitment to friendly governments in the area, particularly Saudi Arabia. The United States seeks not only to promote stability and foster friendly relations, but to ensure its access to oil. Washington has already signaled the Soviet Union that it will not hesitate to use military power, as indicated in the Carter Doctrine, to protect its "vital interests" in the Gulf.

While it is essential for the United States to define its commitment to Gulf security, the formulation and management of an effective policy for the Gulf will be no easy task. The defeat of the Saudi AWACS sale in the House and the political logrolling necessary for its approval in the Senate suggest that the outcome of future votes will by no means be certain. The options open to any administration are likely to be subject to increased domestic political constraints, especially as Gulf security is linked to the Arab-Israeli conflict. Similarly, Gulf states that become closely associated with the United States are likely to experience increasing domestic political pressures that could threaten the legitimacy of their governments. U.S. policymakers thus face a crucial question: To what extent will U.S. policy aimed at protecting the United States' vital interests in the Gulf be compatible with the security interests of the Gulf states? In other words, can U.S. policy be devised that will promote stability and weather the complex rivalries of the Gulf and of the Middle East without violating the sovereign interests of the states in the region or undermining the governments that the United States seeks to uphold?

The purpose of this study is to explore the compatibility of U.S. policy with the security concerns of the Gulf states, with a view to identifying the major problems U.S. policymakers face and to understanding better the prospects for Gulf stability.

Complex Political Relationships

If ever there were an area to which psychologist Else Frenkel-Brunswik's concept of "intolerance of ambiguity" is applicable, it would be the Gulf with its complex and dynamic political relationships. According to Frenkel-Brunswik, as situations become increasingly complex, human beings have a tendency to reduce "frustrating or anxiety-producing uncertainties and contradictions" by oversimplifying them into "neat dichotomous categories—black and white, good and bad, friend and foe."[1]

This phenomenon does not augur well for the success of U.S. policy in the Gulf. The Gulf political context consists of a complex of underlying political conflicts that is complicated by external influences and the linkage of Gulf politics to other, broader conflicts. This creates a situation in which Gulf states can share common interests with the United States on some issues while being in bitter conflict over others. This complicates policy formulation and implementation both in the United States and in the Gulf states.

The number and intensity of the underlying rivalries and conflicts within the Gulf are constantly changing, as are the nature and degree of external involvement. Political relationships in the Gulf are highly complex and interwoven, but can be broken down for the purpose of analysis into four basic types of underlying political conflicts and four broader external conflicts superimposed on the Gulf. The four underlying political conflicts are (1) the struggle between nationalism and imperialism; (2) the struggle between rival nationalisms; (3) the struggle between revolutionary forces and established governments; and (4) the conflict of national interests, usually over territory or resources.[2] The four external conflicts that impact directly on the Gulf are (1) the U.S.-Soviet rivalry; (2) the Arab-Israeli conflict; (3) the conflict between oil-importing and oil-exporting states; and (4) the competition between industrialized states over energy resources and markets.

Underlying Political Conflicts

The struggle between nationalism and imperialism, real or perceived, is ever present in the Gulf. The past memories of British and Russian/Soviet machinations in Iran and the scars left by the French and British Mandates and by the subsequent French and British invasion of Nasser's Egypt create anti-imperialist sentiments throughout the area. More recently, the United States has increasingly become a target of anti-imperialist rhetoric in the Gulf and throughout the Arab world, primarily because of its ties with Israel and with the late Shah of Iran. In the Gulf, Iraq and revolutionary Iran have led the propaganda barrage against the United States, but underlying resentment toward superpower exploitation tends to be widespread. This was apparent when Khomeini's allegations of U.S. involvement in the seizure of the Grand Mosque in Mecca led to an outbreak of anti-American activity. All states in the Gulf are sensitive to any potential threat to their sovereignty and freedom of action and view both superpowers with caution. Gulf states have a lingering fear that the superpowers might attempt to seize the area's resources individually or possibly in concert.[3] Statements made by U.S. officials following the 1973 oil embargo and price rise suggested a possible intervention and contributed to nationalist fears.[4]

The struggle between nationalism and imperialism also has internal dimensions. The nationalist aspirations of many minorities throughout the Gulf, such as the Kurds, the Baluch, and the Dhofaris, among others, represent significant challenges for several governments. The quest for self-determination, whether in the form of increased autonomy or statehood, tends to be vulnerable to political manipulation by outside forces and thus represents a major factor contributing to instability in the region. Other internal dimensions are economic and cultural in character and are reflected in nationalist resentment toward foreign corporations, in particular, and the West, in general. The control of oil production decisions by multinational oil companies in the past is a matter of record; the influences of oil firms today are more subtle, but still open to criticism. The influx of highly paid Westerners (often receiving more pay than nationals for the same work) can sow seeds of hatred, as in Iran's case. Inflation and other economic ills are often associated with foreign business concerns, particularly when there is high visibility and lavish expenditures by Westerners.

The second basic underlying political conflict in the Gulf is the struggle between rival nationalisms. This is represented by the struggle between Iranian nationalism and Arab nationalism. Historically based and having religious and racial overtones, the struggle underlies the Iraq-Iran war. It is also manifest in the bitter dispute over the nomenclature of the Gulf—Is it the Persian Gulf or the Arabian Gulf? All relations between Iran and Arab states are characterized by a certain underlying tension, particularly disputes over boundaries and islands.[5] The Iranian Revolution has had little effect on this underlying conflict, as illustrated by the continuing dispute over the status of Abu Musa and the two Tunb islands and over the name of the Gulf.[6] Iran's Arab neighbors have received the pan-Islamic appeals of Khomeini with distrust, and they continue to doubt Iranian intentions.

The third underlying political conflict tends to be ideological in nature and is represented by the struggle between forces of revolution and established governments seeking to preserve the status quo. Leftist groups, such as Nasserists, Ba'thists, and Communists, have traditionally sought revolutionary change. Presently, the rise of Islamic fundamentalism threatens not only traditional Arab monarchs, but also the nationalist-secular Ba'thist regime of Saddam Hussein in Iraq. It could be argued that Islamic militancy is replacing Marxism and Arab socialism as the number-one driving force for change in the Gulf and throughout the Middle East. In most cases, no clear division of revolutionary forces exists. All work together to overthrow the established order. The anti-imperialist, Fanonian rhetoric that accompanies the various Islamic revolutionary movements appears to be co-opting many student radicals that earlier gravitated toward Marxism.[7] Moreover, many of the Islamic masses throughout the Middle East that were resistant to communist rhetoric are becoming receptive to anti-imperialist, anti-American, anti-Western rhetoric cloaked in an Islamic garb. The success of self-proclaimed Islamic fundamentalists in the Kuwaiti elections in the spring of 1981 suggests that Islamic fundamentalism has a growing political appeal.

The fourth underlying conflict is the struggle between states over questions of national interest and usually involve disputes over territory and resources.[8] These disputes permeate the Gulf and rise or fall in importance depending on the politics of the day. The conflict between Iran and Iraq over the Shatt al-'Arab boundary is an obvious example. Among other ongoing disputes are Iran's control over Abu Musa and the two Tunb islands and Iran's continuing claim to Bahrain. In the northern reaches of the Gulf, the Kuwaitis do not take lightly Iraq's continued interest in Kuwaiti territory and its publicly expressed desire to build a naval base on the Kuwaiti island of Bubiyan.[9] The Kuwaitis remember only too well the earlier Iraqi claim to all of Kuwait. While many of the disputes fluctuate in intensity, others seem to linger with little change. Prospects that an open conflict could erupt are ever present. Moreover, conflicts tend to be susceptible to outside agitation.

Broader External Conflicts

Superimposed on the indigenous conflicts in the Gulf are four broader external conflicts that further complicate the Gulf mosaic. The most threatening to the Gulf states are the U.S.-Soviet rivalry and the Arab-Israeli conflict. The rivalry between oil exporters and oil importers and the competition among Western industrialized states for resources and markets are potentially destabilizing to the global balance and could result in a resort to force in the Gulf.

First, détente did not interrupt the rivalry between the superpowers in the Gulf. While the strategic significance of the Gulf to the two superpowers has changed,[10] the rivalry persists. Initially important because of lines of communication and proximity to the Soviet Union, the Gulf became the oil heartland for the West after 1973. Thus, the United States no longer looked to the Gulf as providing a strategic position relative to the Soviet Union, but had to consider the threat posed to its own economic system if vital energy supplies from the Gulf were cut off.

From the standpoint of the Gulf states, the U.S.-Soviet rivalry remained a pressing concern throughout the postwar period. The Gulf states sought to avoid becoming a battleground for the two superpowers and to escape any superpower presence in the Gulf, especially after the withdrawal of the British from "east of Suez" in 1971. But they have looked to the superpowers for military and technological assistance. The client relationships that developed have raised anew the possibility of proxy wars.

Another outside threat to the Gulf is posed by the possibility of a fifth round in the Arab-Israeli conflict. The June 1981 Israeli raid on the Osirak nuclear reactor near Baghdad suggests that Israel will not hesitate to strike Gulf states if it perceives a serious threat.[11] Israeli concern over Saudi Arabia's growing arms arsenal and over the $8.5 billion AWACS/F-15 enhancement package in particular points to a linkage between the Arab-Israeli conflict and the Gulf.[12] Technological advancement and the acquisition of sophisticated weaponry have given Israel and the Gulf states the capability to target one another in an expanded Arab-Israeli conflict. Moreover, Israeli security concerns and the growth of the Saudi arsenal create a paradox. The Saudi acquisition of sophisticated weaponry provides an effective deterrence to regional disputes and thus promotes stability. When, however, the Saudi weapons acquisition is linked to the Arab-Israeli conflict, it becomes potentially destabilizing. Persistent Israeli overflights of Saudi Arabia and Iraq, such as those reported on 9 November and 30 December 1981 and 3 January 1982,[13] suggest the likelihood of a potentially dangerous air incident.

A different type of rivalry is represented by the conflict of interests between oil-exporting states and oil-importing states. The oil glut on the world market in 1981–82 relaxed tensions over the supply and price of oil, but memories of the 1973 oil embargo will not soon be forgotten. Should the oil states of the Gulf again deny oil to the United States or raise the price exorbitantly, the United States could face increasing domestic pressure to attempt to seize the oil fields.[14] Such a move, of course, would be intricately tied to developments in the area and to the U.S.-Soviet relationship, in particular.

The fourth conflict involving external parties is the competition for limited oil supplies and for expanding markets. This conflict has been evident since 1973 and primarily concerns the Western European states, Japan, and the United States. (It could conceivably extend to other states, including the Soviet Union and the countries of Eastern Europe, as appears to be the case with Iran.) While the industrialized West looks to the Gulf for oil supplies, Western powers appear ready to provide unlimited supplies of sophisticated weaponry and even nuclear technology in return. Not only could this promote regional arms races and threaten to make the Gulf a veritable powder keg, but in times of crisis and extreme competition, it could also undermine the Western alliance system and upset the global balance.

Gulf Security in Perspective

The security equation in the Gulf is complex and involves global and regional balances, as well as questions of national defense and internal security. Gulf security must be viewed as part of a broader U.S. commitment to global security and to the prevention of Soviet aggression. Gulf states, even Iran, cannot ignore such global dimensions of Gulf security, though they are more immediately concerned with regional stability and internal security aspects. While it is clear that many states have security interests in the Gulf, it is not clear which state or states should or will assume responsibility for Gulf security.

Gulf security was the primary responsibility of the British from the early nineteenth century until their withdrawal from "east of Suez" in 1971. The British position came to be augmented (with the cooperation of the United States) by the Baghdad Pact, an alliance system based on the Northern Tier concept.[15] In 1951, before establishment of the Baghdad Pact in1955, Western policymakers sought a "Middle East defense organization," which was to serve as a multilateral defense pact aimed at containing the Soviet Union. Western efforts proved unsuccessful because Egypt and other Arab states were interested more in ridding themselves of the British than in being linked with the British against the Soviets. Subsequently, the Baghdad Pact, later known as the Central Treaty Organization (CENTO), did seek to provide regional security and, presumably with U.S. support, served as a defensive guarantee against Soviet subversion and aggression. U.S. cooperation with CENTO was based on the Mutual Security Act of 1954 and the Eisenhower Doctrine of 1957.[16]

Great Britain's announcement in 1968 of its pending 1971 withdrawal raised the specter of a power vacuum and brought a new U.S. policy response. The Nixon Doctrine, announced on Guam in November 1969, provided that the United States would meet its treaty commitments, and furnish arms and economic assistance to nations threatened by aggression, but would look to such nations to provide the manpower. The United States promised to provide a nuclear shield to protect certain nations vital to its security. The Nixon Doctrine translated into the "twin pillar policy" in the Gulf. The United States provided ever increasing amounts of arms to its regional partners, Iran and Saudi Arabia, and looked to them to provide regional security. Iran became the military pillar and assumed a policing role. Saudi Arabia became the financial pillar and assumed a stabilizing role through the use of financial incentives.

The departure of the Shah in January 1979 signaled the end of this policy and also the breakdown of the broader Northern Tier concept. After Iran announced its intention to withdraw from CENTO in February 1979 and Pakistan did likewise in March, CENTO became defunct. The CENTO headquarters officially closed 26 September 1979.

More shocks to Gulf security came in 1979. U.S. credibility, which had waned in the aftermath of Vietnam[17] and was jolted by the fall of the Shah in January, again suffered with the seizure of the American hostages at the U.S. Embassy in Tehran in November. Later in November, the seizure of the Grand Mosque in Mecca and Khomeini's accusations of U.S. involvement resulted in attacks on U.S. facilities in Pakistan and elsewhere in the Islamic world. In December the Soviet invasion of Afghanistan raised new fears that the Soviet Union might move to the Gulf if not deterred by the expectation of a firm U.S. response.

Thus, at the beginning of the 1980s, the situation in the Gulf, the center of the "arc of crisis,"[18] could be described as one of profound insecurity or precarious stability at best. Gulf security was shaken at every level.

The U.S. Policy Response

The re-evaluation of U.S. Gulf policy at the end of the 1970s was in part a response to the changing strategic relationship between the United States and the Soviet Union. The signing of the SALT II Treaty on 18 June 1979 signaled officially what had been apparent for some time—nuclear parity had been reached. This suggested, at least theoretically, that the U.S. nuclear shield, as guaranteed in the Nixon Doctrine, might no longer extend to conventional conflict. Conventional rearmament was needed to stabilize regional balances of conventional forces to prevent any fait accompli. Secretary of Defense Harold Brown alluded to this when he suggested as early as February 1978 that the United States could no longer "credibly deter" most hostile acts by the threat of nuclear retaliation. In other words, the United States faced the possibility of a Soviet move in the Gulf, especially if there were no conventional forces available to prevent such a move. Out of necessity, the rapid deployment force concept was born. The establishment of the Rapid Deployment Force (RDF) was announced on 5 December 1979.[19]

Carter Doctrine. President Carter in his State of the Union address in January 1980 declared:

> Any attempt by an outside force to gain control of the Persian Gulf region will be regarded as an assault on the vital interests of the United States of America. And such an assault will be repelled by the use of any means necessary including military force.[20]

The statement, known as the Carter Doctrine, signaled to the Soviet Union the willingness of the United States to use force in the Gulf to protect its vital interests. It sought to create the real expectation of U.S. military action if the Soviet Union attempted to seize the Gulf oil fields or cut off the West's vital oil lifeline from the Gulf. Washington underscored the firmness of the commitment by ordering an overflight of the Gulf by B-52 strategic bombers in January 1980 following Soviet troop movements near Iran.

The Carter Doctrine was to be backed up with the newest military option, the RDF. The RDF had been in planning stages for several years and was intended to enhance the U.S. military presence in the Middle East. Initially it was to consist of three Marine brigades of 5500 each to be ready by 1983.[21] Presumably, if a crisis called for the use of force, the RDF would be airlifted to designated areas, joined with pre-positioned sea-based and land-based equipment, and be ready for combat in a minimum amount of time. The RDF was closely associated with the "over the horizon" fleet concept, but still depended on access to air bases and port facilities. Accordingly, the United States actively sought facilities-access agreements with states bordering the Indian Ocean. In 1980 it reached agreements with Kenya (April), Oman (June), and Somalia (August), but not with Egypt or Saudi Arabia. Egypt offered the use of facilities on a temporary basis, however, and the two states reportedly reached an informal arrangement allowing the United States to use facilities on the Ras Banas peninsula. Egypt had balked at any U.S. base on Egyptian soil. Similarly, Saudi Arabia would not permit U.S. combat forces in Saudi Arabia. Washington planned to expand U.S. facilities at Diego Garcia for RDF use.

The Carter Doctrine and the RDF brought loud outcries from the Gulf and sharp criticism and hard questions from within the United States. The Gulf states were highly suspicious and charged that the Carter Doctrine was a pretext for intervention in the area. Saudi Arabia proved to be an exception, however; then Crown Prince Fahd reportedly supported the thrust of the Carter Doctrine.

Domestic critics were relentless in their attack. They charged that the United States did not have the conventional military forces to confront any Soviet move. They questioned the viability of the RDF, insisting it could not be deployed rapidly and was not a force. Military officials and President Carter were quick to acknowledge that the United States did lack the military strength to defend the Gulf unilaterally. This led to a realization that the RDF, as initially constituted, was little more than a "tripwire," probably backed by a nuclear response.[22] Two other major criticisms of the RDF focused on "the lack of secure military access in the region" and the RDF's dependence on forces committed elsewhere.[23] The Congressional Staff Study Mission to the Persian Gulf (21 October to 13 November 1980) went so far as to question "whether U.S. security needs in the Persian Gulf can be accomplished adequately short of a permanent American military presence in the area."[24]

Regardless of the criticism, the Carter Doctrine informed the world of the United States' resolve to use force to protect its vital interests in the Gulf. Despite some conflicting signals from administration officials, it was directed at Soviet actions only and was not intended (at least initially) to encompass use of U.S. armed forces in regional or internal conflicts. The United States still looked to regional partners to provide their own internal security and to defend against external attack, while promising to intervene to stop Soviet aggression. The United States did not turn to a new regional partner to assume Iran's stabilizing role in the Gulf. Washington apparently considered Egypt,[25] but its alienation from the Gulf because of its participation in the Camp David process precluded such a possibility.[26] Instead, the United States continued to rely on security assistance to bolster friendly governments. The arms sales were augmented, as necessary, with the deployment of U.S. naval forces to the area, "fly-ins," and joint military exercises.

The Soviet Union responded to the increased U.S. activity in the area by proposing a "doctrine of peace and security." On 10 December 1980 Brezhnev called on the world powers to agree not to set up bases or bring nuclear weapons into the area. The following day a joint Soviet-Indian declaration was signed, calling for the dismantling of all foreign bases in the area, including the U.S. facility at Diego Garcia. Washington rejected the plan. U.S. officials quickly pointed to the presence of Soviet troops in Afghanistan as the principal threat to Gulf security.

Strategic Concensus. When the Reagan administration took office, it did not attempt to change the basic policy direction set forth by the Carter Doctrine but emphasized the need to balance change with consistency.[27] Facing a continuing "window of vulnerability" with the Soviet Union, a Camp David peace process that was losing momentum, and a U.S. credibility problem in the Gulf that had worsened since the abortive attempt to rescue the American hostages, the Reagan administration moved strongly to rebuild the United States' conventional and nuclear strength to improve the global strategic balance. In the Middle East, the United States moved to improve its credibility by identifying the Soviet Union as the greatest threat, projecting a strong commitment to friendly governments, and taking a hard line on terrorism.

The thrust of the new policy became known as "strategic consensus." As Secretary of State Alexander Haig explained:

> In Southwest Asia, the United States is seeking a strategic consensus among our friends directed toward the common Soviet threat. We are attempting to convince them that we are a reliable and capable security partner, serious about defending our vital interests in the region in partnership with them.[28]

The emphasis on the Soviet Union as the "common threat" was directed at the strengthening of security partnerships throughout the Middle East, from Israel and Egypt to the Gulf states. Presumably, stronger partnerships would enable the United States to increase its military presence throughout the region. The aim of this policy was to deter Soviet aggression and possibly adventuristic acts by Soviet clients, while bolstering friendly governments and strengthening their resolve to deal with external opposition, internal subversion, and revolution.

To support its emphasis on the Soviet Union as the common threat, the Reagan administration revised its conception of a quick-strike force. In April

1981, plans were announced for a new permanent military command to protect vital U.S. interests in the Gulf. The Rapid Deployment Joint Task Force (RDJTF), as the RDF came to be called, was to be much larger and fully independent, not depending on troops committed elsewhere. The RDJTF was transformed into a new unified command, the U.S. Central Command (US CENTCOM), on 1 January 1983. It was to consist of over 200,000 troops by 1983, and possibly over 400,000 by 1985. Washington also decided that the RDJTF could respond to any circumstance in which "the security of access to Persian Gulf oil is threatened."[29]

AWACS/F-15 Enhancement Sale. Two major policy initiatives in the fall of 1981 were linked to "strategic consensus": the AWACS/F-15 enhancement sale in October and the U.S.-Israeli "strategic memorandum" in November. The AWACS package was aimed at restoring U.S. credibility in the Gulf and was viewed as a crucial litmus test for broader U.S.-Saudi relations.[30] The $8.5 billion AWACS package consisted of 5 E-3A AWACS aircraft, 202 (101 sets) conformal fuel tanks for F-15 aircraft, 1,177 AIM-9L Sidewinder air-to-air missiles, and 8 Boeing 707 aerial refueling aircraft. Purportedly, the AWACS package would improve Saudi defenses against threats emanating from several regional sources, among which were identified a spillover of the Iraq-Iran war and threats of attacks from South Yemen and Ethiopia (each having a Soviet military presence).[31] The AWACS package was also tied in part to the Soviet Union. It was intended to facilitate any necessary U.S. reinforcement in response to a Soviet attack. Perhaps the most important aspect of the AWACS package would be its enhancement of the Saudi capability to defend oil fields against air attacks from regional powers. Not only would the AWACS provide early warning, but the conformal fuel tanks and the AIM-9L missiles would greatly improve the firepower and range of the Saudi F-15 aircraft, the Carter administration's 1978 assurances to the Israelis notwithstanding. (The first group of Saudi F-15 fighter aircraft arrived in Saudi Arabia on 18 January 1982, piloted by Saudis.)[32] The AIM-9L missiles would give the Saudi F-15s an important head-on attack capability.

The impact of the AWACS sale is likely to extend for years to come because the sale promises to entail U.S. involvement with the Saudi AWACS operations beyond 1990. The Israeli reaction to the AWACS package, however, raises some uncertainties for both U.S.-Israeli relations and for the future of the United States' Gulf policy.

The Reagan administration apparently did not foresee the intensity of the Israeli reaction. The administration had asserted that the sale would not significantly affect Israel's military superiority throughout the region and, in the long run, would contribute to stability in the Gulf, and thus to Israel's security. The immediate Israeli reaction, however, suggested that Israel was far more concerned about the political implications of the sale and a possible U.S. tilt toward Saudi Arabia, which could directly impact on Israeli security as Israelis perceived it. The degree of their concern was underscored by Israel's harsh response to the eight-point Fahd Plan, which President Reagan positively acknowledged soon after the Senate approval of the AWACS sale.[33] Israeli prime minister Menachim Begin not only condemned the plan point by point, but also warned that its consideration could undermine the Camp David peace process.

The unusually strong Israeli stance against the AWACS sale and against Saudi Arabia will undoubtedly impact on the policy process within the United States and will influence domestic perceptions of Saudi Arabia.[34] The AWACS sale passed by a close Senate vote, 52–48, after being overwhelmingly defeated in the House. Future votes on U.S. policy in the Gulf could surely be contentious, especially if Israel were aligned against the administration.

Strategic Memorandum with Israel. A month after the approval of the AWACS sale of Saudi Arabia, the United States and Israel agreed on a "memorandum of understanding." This formal agreement, based on the Reagan administration's policy of strategic concensus, provided for strategic cooperation against Soviet threats and threats caused by "Soviet-controlled" forces from "outside the region." It purposefully did not identify threats other than those emanating from the Soviet Union and specifically provided that "the strategic cooperation is not directed at any state or group of states within the Middle East." The agreement provided for joint air and naval exercises but not land exercises, thus avoiding U.S. troops on Israeli territory. The agreement showed a U.S. sensitivity to the views of moderate Arab leaders and fell short of Israeli expectations. Israel reportedly had envisioned a much greater degree of cooperation.[35]

The United States subsequently suspended the strategic memorandum on 18 December 1981, following Israel's annexation of the Golan Heights. Prime Minister Begin responded with an emotional outburst against the United States and asserted that the memorandum was canceled. The following week, however, Defense Minister Ariel Sharon maintained that the strategic memorandum was still in force.

Question of Direction. Nicholas A. Veliotes, assistant secretary for Near Eastern and South Asian affairs, has explained that U.S. policy toward the Middle East and Persian Gulf has two central themes—the search for peace and the search for security.[36] Each is intricately related to the other. Secretary of State Haig spoke of a "comprehensive strategy," a "strategy that neglects neither regional complexities nor the threat of external intervention,"[37] and explained that "the United States regards the peace process and the effort to counter Soviet and regional threats as mutually reinforcing."[38] While it is apparent that U.S. policy seeks to be comprehensive in approach and responsive to regional complexities, questions have arisen whether a policy based on a "consensus of strategic concern" and emphasizing the immediacy of the Soviet threat is too narrow for the subtleties of the Gulf political context. In particular, is "strategic consensus" an adequate vehicle for establishing and maintaining regional partnerships to the degree necessary to allow continued U.S. access to oil supplies and a possible defense of the oil fields? Is there an overemphasis on the Soviet threat at the expense of other threats?[39] In terms of Gulf security, is a policy that emphasizes the Soviet threat compatible with the security interests of the Gulf states?

The Gulf States' Response

The search for security after the fall of the Shah has varied from state to state, but the Gulf states have primarily focused on regional threats and internal security. The Carter Doctrine and strategic consensus notwithstanding, the Gulf states have tended not to perceive an immediate Soviet threat. Oman, to a degree, represents an exception, possibly because of its strategic location on the Strait of Hormuz.[40] Its sensitivity to the Soviet threat made it more receptive to U.S. overtures for a facilities-access agreement. The threats emanating from the revolutionary pressures spawned by the Iranian Revolution seem more serious to the other Gulf states. Iran's efforts to sow revolution, together with a lingering border dispute, brought an armed response from Iraq in September 1980. The remaining Gulf states moved to improve their security through increased cooperation, especially through the Gulf Cooperation Council (GCC), formally organized in February 1981. The Gulf sheikhdoms gravitated toward Saudi Arabia to seek protection from the possible spillover of the Iraq-Iran war and from subversion and revolution spread by Iran. Saudi Arabia has been especially interested in expanding security cooperation with the smaller Gulf states since the Grand Mosque seizure. In this regard, a threat to one state has been increasingly viewed as a threat to all.[41]

In addition to their concerns about regional threats and internal security, Saudi Arabia and other Gulf states have come to view Israel as an integral part of their security problem. They not only perceive a threat of an Israeli attack,[42] but also believe that their policy on Israel and Palestinian rights is a principal ingredient in domestic stability, both because of their broader Arab and Islamic ties with front-line Arab states and because of the presence of a large Palestinian population in much of the Arab Gulf.[43]

Reaction to Regional Threats. The major thrust of the Gulf states' response to regional threats, as indicated by Saudi Arabia, is to "go it alone," to build a military capability that is not dependent on any outside power. Accordingly, Saudi Arabia turned to the acquisition of sophisticated arsenals from diverse sources to create an independent long-term defensive capability.[44] The AWACS/F-15 enhancement sale to Saudi Arabia was to serve such a purpose. In the near term, Saudi Arabia has looked to emergency large-scale transfers of U.S. weaponry, such as funded by Saudi Arabia for North Yemen in 1979. Saudi Arabia has also welcomed visits by U.S. airpower, an over-the-horizon presence of U.S. naval power, and the loan of four AWACS aircraft (prior to the AWACS/F-15 enhancement sale), presumably to promote stability in the Gulf.

Despite looking to U.S. assistance in the near term, Saudi Arabia adamantly refuses to be linked to the United States in any defensive alliance and strongly opposes any U.S. military presence or base rights in the area. Prince Saud, the Saudi foreign minister, asserted at the Ta'if Conference in 1979 that the responsibility for Gulf security and defense "lies exclusively with the Gulf countries."[45] At the Third Islamic Summit in January 1981, Crown Prince Fahd, reading a statement from King Khalid, urged all Muslim countries to resist military alliances with the superpowers.[46] In November 1981, Prince Saud strongly criticized Oman for its participation in the RDJTF exercise Operation Bright Star II. Prince Saud called Oman's participation contrary to the Gulf states' principle of nonalignment. Moreover, reports indicate that the other Gulf states offered incentives to Oman to revoke its facilities-access agreement with the United States.[47]

An attack on a GCC state became a reality on 1 October 1981, when Iranian aircraft reportedly bombed some Kuwaiti oil facilities, causing extensive damage. Shortly thereafter, in mid-November, the GCC reportedly agreed to create an air defense system that incorporated AWACS radar planes "for the collective defense of the Gulf."[48] In February 1982, during Secretary of Defense Caspar Weinberger's visit, Saudi Arabia requested sophisticated air defense equipment and indicated a desire to coproduce weapons in the Gulf. Meetings of GCC defense ministers and interior ministers in early 1982 suggested that cooperation to "ensure regional security against external threats" was continuing.[49]

Apart from strictly defensive measures, the security interests of the GCC have been promoted through diplomatic measures, such as the mediation of regional disputes. GCC efforts aimed at the renewal of relations between Saudi Arabia and Libya contributed to a lessening of tensions between the GCC and the Aden Pact (Libya, Ethiopia, and South Yemen). Similar efforts directed at defusing the friction between Oman and South Yemen have been noteworthy.

Internal Security Measures. Cooperation promises to strengthen the collective defense of the GCC states, but the GCC is focusing even greater attention on internal security. The entire Gulf is aware that the Shah's downfall came from within, not from any external attack. Major efforts to promote the legitimacy of incumbent governments and strengthen internal security are occurring throughout the Gulf. States have emphasized the Islamic dimension of their governments,[50] promised increased political participation, and provided generously for the general welfare of their nationals to curb domestic pressures and to enhance their legitimacy.[51] At the same time, they are taking new steps to modernize internal security forces with the most advanced equipment,[52] as well as to increase cooperation through bilateral security agreements and possibly a collective security pact.

Much attention was focused on internal security after the Grand Mosque incident, but the real catalyst for internal security cooperation was the discovery of the Bahrain sabotage plot on 13 December 1981. The Bahrain plot, undertaken by the Islamic Front for the Liberation of Bahrain, involved direct Iranian participation in the attempt to overthrow the government of Bahrain and an apparent saboteur network that extended into other states. With such potentially volatile groups as the Shi'as and the various immigrant groups throughout the Gulf susceptible to outside revolutionary pressure,[53] Saudi Arabia and the other GCC states moved forthrightly and creatively to bolster their security relations.

Saudi Arabia and Bahrain signed a bilateral security agreement on 20 December 1981 that provided for the organization of their security relations, coordination between Interior ministries, extradition of criminals, and coordination on all security matters.[54] Similar Saudi treaties were reportedly drafted with Kuwait and Qatar, with the possibility that all of them might eventually be linked. In addition to the bilateral treaties, Bahraini interior minister Sheikh Mohammed ibn Khalifah al-Khalifah called for joint cooperation to form a GCC rapid deployment force.[55] The Saudi interior minister, Prince Nayif, stated that, if they were ever requested, Saudi security forces would be in any Gulf country in a very short time.[56] Such actions illustrate the determination of Saudi Arabia and the GCC to respond to threats to their internal security quickly and without looking to outside powers for support.[57]

Response to an Israeli Threat. The use of the oil weapon by Saudi Arabia and other Gulf states in 1973 signaled a more active involvement in the Arab-Israeli conflict. Since then, Saudi Arabia and other Gulf states have been active diplomatically, seeking the return of occupied Arab land, including East Jerusalem, and the restoration of the legitimate rights of the Palestinian people. While it is beyond the scope of this study to detail the many policies of the Gulf states that deal with Israel and with the Palestinians,[58] it is important to note that Arab charges of "Zionist imperialism" and "aggression," though in part for domestic consumption,[59] are not viewed as idle rhetoric. The Gulf states perceive a real threat of Israeli attack. Iraq undoubtedly believes that Israel could strike again, especially if the nuclear reactor near Baghdad is rebuilt. Accordingly, the Gulf states see their security preparations as a response to an Israeli threat (in spite of the threat assessment sent to Congress with the AWACS package). For example, Prince Fahd asserted in January 1982 that the Saudi AWACS "will deprive Israel of the element of surprise whenever it wants to attack any Arab country."[60]

Problems

U.S. policymakers, like those of the Gulf states, are caught in a paradox. The United States and the Gulf states are well aware that the latter could not defend themselves against a Soviet attack, but the Gulf states remain committed to avoiding a U.S. presence in the Gulf. If, as one critic has suggested, the utility of the RDJTF turns on "the lack of secure military access ashore in the region"[61] and U.S. ground access is not welcome, then security remains questionable and ad hoc at best.

The question of why the United States would not be welcome is complex, but is based on a perception of the United States as an imperialist power and an ally of Israel.[62] Most significant at present is the United States' support for and identification with Israel and its hostility toward the Palestine Liberation Organization.[63] Thus, the present U.S. search for a strategic consensus is reminiscent of the earlier search for a Middle East defense organization. Then the Americans attempted to link Egypt and other Arab states with the British against a Soviet threat, but had little success because the Arabs were more concerned with ridding themselves of the British. Today, the Arab Gulf states are concerned more with Israel than with the Soviet Union. The subtleties of the U.S. strategic memorandum with Israel and the fact that the agreement fell short of Israeli expectations were lost on the Arab masses.

The two basic problems facing U.S. policy in terms of compatibility of U.S. views on Gulf security with those of the Gulf states—the determination of the Gulf states to avoid any U.S. military presence in the Gulf and the growing perception of the United States as a pro-Israeli, imperialist power—have serious implications for the future of Gulf security.

First, they signal that the Arab-Israeli conflict is firmly linked to the Gulf, not only from the technological-military viewpoint but also a political viewpoint. Perceptions are dichotomous and subject to emotional prejudice, giving rise to intolerance of ambiguity. The United States' actions throughout the Gulf are suspect to Arabs because of its relationship with Israel. Conversely, U.S. actions to promote the defensive capability of Gulf states, such as the

AWACS sale, are suspect to the Israelis. The domestic political pressures in the United States unleashed by the AWACS/F-15 enhancement sale and fanned by Israel can only limit U.S. policy options and create doubt that the United States could act definitively in a crisis. The not-so-subtle conflict among scholars and analysts over the intentions of Saudi Arabia and Israel have generated threat assessments that can only be called political exercises.

Second, closely related to the Arab perception of U.S.-Israeli collusion is the movement of the Gulf states toward a negative—from the U.S. viewpoint—nonalignment caused by increasing domestic pressures. U.S.-Israeli ties increasingly force the Saudi and other Gulf governments to detach themselves from close cooperation with the United States for fear of undermining their own legitimacy. This drift toward a negative nonalignment, with its anti-American rhetoric, could be very damaging to U.S. interests in the Gulf. The exhortations of the Kuwaiti National Assembly, calling on "Arab states to close ranks against the American-Israeli alliance,"[64] do not augur well for U.S. interests, especially if political participation increases and media hostility toward the United States is allowed. Dangers implicit in the growing popularity of anti-American rhetoric not only create problems for the implementation of joint exercises, such as Operation Bright Star II, but also could lead Saudi Arabia and other Gulf states to become more receptive to Soviet overtures to re-establish (or establish for the first time) diplomatic relations. Maintaining relations with both superpowers could minimize the political costs of receiving military assistance from one.

Third, those seeking to use anti-American sentiments to undermine the stability of incumbent governments and sour their relations with the United States could play on countervailing pressures resulting from large-scale arms sales. Perhaps no aspect of U.S. Gulf policy has been subjected to more criticism than arms sales. This is partly because of the effects of the influx of advisers and technical support personnel and partly because of the stigma of becoming a "client" of a superpower. Isolationist tendencies within the United States are concerned that too many advisers can draw the United States into entangling alliances and unwanted wars. Moreover, the very presence of large numbers of foreigners can place in question a state's independence and bring charges of imperialism, as well as blame for all the frustrations of a developing society. The United States may not seek to "engulf the Gulf" with advisers, facilities, or excessive military hardware,[65] but any U.S. arms transfer will have a political cost even if Americans maintain a minimal visibility.

Fourth, Iran's efforts to export revolution in the Gulf will undoubtedly target governments that are associated with the United States. These efforts could become a serious threat to vital U.S. interests. Iranian efforts to spread revolution through anti-American rhetoric in Islamic sermons, blatant misinformation broadcast throughout the Gulf, and covert plots, such as uncovered in Bahrain, promise to be only a beginning. The threat of Iranian armed intervention is likely to increase as Iran gains the upper hand in the Gulf war, especially if Iran is able to neutralize Iraq. Reports that Iranian hovercraft "loaded with troops and equipment" were "standing ready" to assist the Bahraini saboteurs[66] are only too believable when it is remembered that the Shah's hovercraft fleet gave Iran a Gulf-wide quick-strike capability as early as 1973.[67] The bold calls for the overthrow of the Saudi government broadcast from Iran in early February 1982 could be interpreted as a harbinger of armed intervention to liberate fellow Muslims from the yoke of U.S. "imperialism," especially the large Shi'a population near the Ras Tanura oil fields, which are readily accessible from the Gulf. Moreover, devout Iranian Islamic revolutionaries could just as easily attack the oil fields in Saudi Arabia to strike at the heart of the Western "imperialist" economic system as could any devout communist, and probably without threatening nuclear war. An emergent, uncompromising Iran, possibly strengthened by a victory in its war with Iraq, could cause increasing threats to the United States and to Gulf security.

The United States has created a clear expectation that it will use force in the Gulf to counter any aggressive Soviet attack, but the United States must continue to upgrade its military capability and especially its conventional forces to maintain the precarious global strategic balance and restore the regional conventional balance in the Gulf.

The United States has attempted to improve its credibility with Saudi Arabia and other Gulf states through the sale of sophisticated weaponry, temporary visits from U.S. air and sea power, and the building of a rapid deployment force, which remains over the horizon at present. The United States has not, however, responded to threats to its interests and the undercutting of its credibility in the Gulf caused by the perception of the United States as a pro-Israeli, imperialist power. It must act to counter such perceptions through a responsible policy dedicated to principle and flexible enough to deal openly with all parties including the Palestinians and the Israelis. Positive action acknowledging that the Arab-Israeli conflict is firmly linked to U.S. security concerns in the Gulf is necessary.

Finally, the United States needs to take the initiative to combat misinformation and improve how it is perceived in the Gulf. More specifically, the United States should not assume that negative nonalignment, with its anti-U.S. rhetoric, is acceptable because it is also presumably anti-Soviet. The denial of access and threats of revolutionary measures against U.S. interests are just as damaging when they came from Tehran or Tripoli as when they originate in Moscow. Even in the absence of Soviet involvement, Washington should perceive an anti-U.S. revolutionary state as a threat.

Notes

1. See Else Frenkel-Brunswik, "Intolerance of Ambiguity as an Emotional and Perceptual Personality Variable," *Journal of Personality* 18 (September 1949): 108–43.

2. For an analysis of the political dynamics of the Gulf from the standpoint of Iran, see Charles G. MacDonald, "Iran as a Political Variable: Patterns and Prospects," in Enver M. Koury and Charles G. MacDonald, eds., *Revolution in Iran: A Reappraisal* (Washington, D.C.: Institute of Middle Eastern and North African Affairs, 1982), pp. 49–60.

3. Shafqat Ali Shah asserts that a school of thought widespread in the area "believes that not only the Soviet Union, but the United States as well, have designs on the area," and that "the two superpowers may well come to collaborate in absorbing the vital resources of the area into their respective spheres of influence and control" ("Southwest Asia: Can the US Learn from Past Mistakes?" *Strategic Review* 9 [Winter 1981]: 27–35).

4. For statements made by President Ford, Secretary of State Henry Kissinger, and Secretary of Defense James Schlesinger, see U.S. Congress, House of Representatives, Committee on International Relations, *Oil Fields as Military Objectives: A Feasibility Study* (Washington, D.C.: Government Printing Office, 1975), pp. 77–82.

5. See Will D. Swearingen, "Sources of Conflict over Oil in the Persian/Arabian Gulf," *Middle East Journal* 35 (1981): 315–30.

6. In March 1980 Abolhasan Bani-Sadr stated in an interview with Beirut's *an-Nahar* that Iran did not plan to give up the three Gulf islands claimed by the Arab states and was not interested in good relations with the Arab states of the "Persian Gulf" (see *New York Times*, 29 March 1980).

7. For example, one Iranian student who supported a leftist group told me that some of his fellow leftists had begun to support the fundamentalist Islamic Republican party in Iran because of its anti-imperialist rhetoric.

8. For the identification of some 38 disputes, see Charles G. MacDonald, *Iran, Saudi Arabia, and the Law of Sea: Political Interaction and Legal Development in the Persian Gulf* (Westport, Conn.: Greenwood Press, 1980), pp. 33–36. See also S. H. Amin, *International and Legal Problems of the Gulf* (London: Menas Press, 1981); and Ali A. El-Hakim, *The Middle Eastern States and the Law of the Sea* (Syracuse, N.Y.: Syracuse University Press, 1979), pp. 83–131.

9. See *Middle East Economic Digest* (London), 25 (17/23 July 1981): 21.

10. For U.S. interests, see Robert G. Irani (Darius), "US Strategic Interests in Iran and Saudi Arabia," *Parameters* 7 (December 1977): 21–34; and U.S. Congress, House of Representatives, Committee on Foreign Affairs, *US Security Interests in the Persian Gulf* (Washington, D.C.: Government Printing Office, 1981). For an overview of Soviet interests and policies, see Alvin Z. Rubinstein, "The Evolution of Soviet Strategy in the Middle East," *Orbis* 24 (1980): 323–37; and Dennis Ross,

"Considering Soviet Threats to the Persian Gulf," *International Security* 6, no. 2 (Fall 1981): 159–80.

11. For an Israeli strategic perspective, see Youhannan Ramati, "The Strategic Balance in the Middle East: Effect of the Iran-Iraq War," *Midstream* 27 (August/ September 1981): 3–6. See also U.S. Congress, House of Representatives, Committee on Foreign Relations, *Israeli Attack on Iraqi Nuclear Facilities* (Washington, D.C.: Government Printing Office, 1981).

12. See U.S. Congress, Senate, Committee on Foreign Relations, *The Proposed AWACS/F-15 Enhancement Sale to Saudi Arabia* (Washington, D.C.: Government Printing Office, 1981).

13. For accounts of such overflights, see *Foreign Broadcast Information Service (FBIS)*, *Middle East and Africa*, 10 November 1981, p. C-1, and 4 January 1982, p. E-1.

14. See Robert W. Tucker, "Oil: The Issue of American Intervention," *Commentary* 59 (January 1975): 21–31.

15. The Northern Tier concept, raised in 1953 by John Foster Dulles, sought to link the states on the southern periphery of the Soviet Union into a defensive alliance or "collective security system." See Rouhollah K. Ramazani, *The Northern Tier: Afghanistan, Iran and Turkey* (Princeton, N.J.: Van Nostrand, 1966), p. 3.

16. See Ralph H. Magnus, "International Organization in the Persian Gulf," in Alvin J. Cottrell et al., eds., *The Persian Gulf States: A General Survey* (Baltimore, Md.: Johns Hopkins University Press, 1980), pp. 172–91.

17. For the adverse effect Vietnam had on U.S. credibility in the Gulf in the mid-1970s, see Abbas Amirie, "Introduction," in idem, ed., *The Persian Gulf and the Indian Ocean in International Politics* (Tehran: Institute for International Political and Economic Studies, 1975), p. 3.

18. See George Lenczowski, "The Arc of Crisis: Its Central Sector," *Foreign Affairs* 57 (1978/79): 796–820.

19. See George C. Wilson, "Marines to Form Rapid Reaction Force," *Washington Post*, 6 December 1979.

20. For text, see *New York Times*, 24 January 1980.

21. See Maxwell O. Johnson, "US Strategic Options in the Persian Gulf," *US Naval Institute Proceedings* 107 (February 1981): 53–59.

22. See David D. Newsom, "America Engulfed," *Foreign Policy*, no. 43 (Summer 1981): 17–32; and Joshua M. Epstein, "Soviet Vulnerabilities in Iran and the RDF Deterrent," *International Security* 6, no. 2 (Fall 1981): 126–58.

23. For a penetrating analysis of a computerized war game Gallant Knight, which involved a mock attempt by the U.S. Readiness Command to block a Soviet invasion of Iran's oil area, see Jeffrey Record, "Disneyland Planning for the Persian Gulf Oil Defense," *Washington Star*, 20 March 1981. See also idem, "The Rapid Deployment Force: Problems, Constraints, and Needs," *Annals of the American Academy of Political and Social Science* 457 (September 1981): 109–20.

24. House of Representatives, Committee on Foreign Affairs, *US Security Interests in the Persian Gulf*, p. 13.

25. Professor Rouhallah K. Ramazani's classic study of Gulf security raises the question, "Who should maintain the future security of the Persian Gulf?" His case for an indigenous regional security arrangement has had a major impact on the Gulf. ("Security in the Persian Gulf," *Foreign Affairs* 57 [1978/79]: 821–35.)

26. Egyptian arms transfers to Iraq reported in early 1981 suggest that a rapprochement with the Gulf states could be forthcoming.

27. See U.S. Department of State, Bureau of Public Affairs, "US Strategy in the Middle East," *Current Policy* (Washington, D.C.: Government Printing Office), 312 (17 September 1981): 1.

28. For Secretary Haig's remarks before the Senate Armed Services Committee, see U.S. Department of State, Bureau of Public Affairs, "Relationship of Foreign and Defense Policies," *Current Policy* 320 (30 July 1981): 3.

29. For a discussion of the five-year U.S. defense master plan reported in May 1982, see Richard Halloran, "Special U.S. Force for Persian Gulf Is Growing Swiftly," *New York Times*, 25 October 1982; see also Charles G. MacDonald, "The United States and Gulf Conflict Scenarios," *Middle East Insight* 3 (May–July 1983): 23–27.

30. The damage to U.S. credibility in the Gulf resulting from a defeat of the proposed AWACS sale would have been much greater than any benefit gained from its passage.

31. See address of Joseph W. Twinam, deputy assistant secretary for Near Eastern and South Asian affairs, before the National Conference of Editorial Writers, in U.S. Department of State, Bureau of Public Affairs, "Saudi Arabia and US Security Policy," *Current Policy* 320 (25 September 1981): 2.

32. *FBIS*, 18 January 1982, p. C-8.

33. The Reagan administration initially interpreted the eight-point Fahd Plan, put forward on 8 August 1981, as nothing more than a restatement of U.N. resolutions. Later, the administration emphasized an implicit recognition of Israel in point 7, which affirms the right of all countries of the region to live in peace.

34. For an apparent polarization developing among writers on Saudi Arabia, see J. B. Kelly and Hermann F. Eilts, "Point/Counterpoint," *International Security* 5, no. 4 (Spring 1981): 186–203.

35. For the Israeli position, see Wolf Blitzer, "The Strategic Deal with Israel," *Jerusalem Post* (weekly international edition), 13/19 September 1981.

36. See U.S. Department of State, Bureau of Public Affairs, "Pursuing Peace and Security in the Middle East," *Current Policy* 322 (21 October 1981): 1.

37. See U.S. Department of State, "US Strategy in the Middle East," p. 2.

38. Ibid.

39. Ambassador Christopher Van Hollen asserts that the most immediate threat to the cutoff of oil from the Persian Gulf is not the Soviet Union but regional actors, as

evidenced by previous interruptions—the OPEC embargo, the Iranian Revolution, and the Iraq-Iran war. Moreover, a May 1981 revision of the 1977 CIA assessment of oil so influential in weighing the Soviet threat indicates Soviet oil production will be much greater than anticipated. A CIA study, reported 3 September 1981, similarly projected that the Soviet Union would be an oil exporter "for the immediate future," thus suggesting that at least one interest pushing the Soviet Union in the direction of the Gulf is not as significant as earlier believed. (See Christopher Van Hollen, "Weinberger's Specter," *New York Times*, 4 October 1981.)

40. It might also be argued that Iran, in January 1980, also was an exception because of its fears of a possible Soviet intervention.

41. This concept of "collective Arab security" has appeared repeatedly in statements of Gulf officials after the Bahraini sabotage plot was uncovered. For an earlier identification of "collective Arab security" in a reported Saudi security plan, see "Gulf Security Document," *Middle East* (London) 75 (January 1981): 16–17.

42. Israel has suggested that in any fifth round of the Arab-Israeli war, the Arab states that fund Arab war efforts will not be immune from attack.

43. For the Saudi emphasis on the Palestinian issue, see William B. Quandt, "Riyadh Between the Superpowers," *Foreign Policy*, no. 44 (Fall 1981): 41; and idem, *Saudi Arabia in the 1980s: Foreign Policy, Security, and Oil* (Washington, D.C.: Brookings Institute, 1982).

44. For a discussion of Saudi defense considerations, see Charles G. MacDonald, "Reactions to Iran's Revolution: The Search for Security," in Koury and MacDonald, *Revolution in Iran: A Reappraisal,* pp. 99–103. See also Adeed I. Dawisha, "Saudi Arabia's Search for Security," *Adelphi Papers*, no. 158 (Winter 1979–80): 250.

45. *Arab News* (Jeddah), 18 October 1971.

46. See Pranay B. Gupte, "King Khalid Entreats Islamic Leaders to Shun Alliances with Superpowers," *New York Times*, 26 January 1981.

47. *Washington Post*, 2 December 1981.

48. The sharing of information picked up by the AWACS, though carefully provided for in the agreement, promises to be a continuing point of contention between Saudi Arabia and the United States (see *FBIS*, 13 November 1981, p. C-1).

49. Ibid., 29 December 1981, p. C-3.

50. For a penetrating study of the use of Islam to legitimize the Saudi government and combat radical pan-Arabism, see James P. Piscatori, "The Formation of the Saudi Identity: A Case Study of the Utility of Transnationalism," in John F. Stack, Jr., ed., *Ethnic Identities in a Transnational World* (Westport, Conn.: Greenwood Press, 1981), pp. 105–40.

51. See MacDonald, "Reactions to Iran's Revolution," pp. 98–109.

52. The Saudi "computer-assisted surveillance system" with branches at various points of entry is an obvious example, see "Gulf Unity: Building in Progress," *Middle East* (London) 78 (April 1981): 8–9.

53. For an examination of internal factors in the United Arab Emirates, see John Duke Anthony, "Transformation Amidst Tradition: The United Arab Emirates in

Transition," in Shahram Chubin, ed., *Security in the Persian Gulf*, vol. 1, *Domestic Political Factors*, (Montclair, N.J.: Allanheld, Osmun, 1981), pp. 19–37.

54. *FBIS*, 22 December 1981, p. C-2.

55. Ibid., 7 January 1982, p. C-2.

56. Perhaps the Saudi Special Security Force (SSF) could respond, at least on a small scale. A large-scale operation would require outside assistance, possibly from Jordanian, Pakistani, or even Egyptian forces. (See ibid., 22 December 1981, p. C-2.)

57. If backup support were needed, it would be sought from within the region, at least at first. President Reagan is on record as offering U.S. intervention to prevent Saudi Arabia from having the same fate as Iran. His statements in early October 1981 forecast a "Reagan doctrine" if such a threat should materialize.

58. For a comprehensive study on the Palestinians, see John W. Amos, II, *Palestinian Resistance: Organization of a Nationalist Movement* (New York: Pergamon Press, 1980).

59. Gulf leaders are very much aware that the Palestinians present in the Gulf represent a potential revolutionary threat.

60. *FBIS*, 8 January 1982, p. C-2.

61. Jeffrey Record, "The RDF: Is the Pentagon Kidding?" *Washington Quarterly* 4 (Summer 1981): 41–51.

62. As Ambassador Hermann F. Eilts points out, "perceptions count in the Gulf" ("Security Considerations in the Persian Gulf," *International Security* 5, no. 2 [Fall 1980]: 82).

63. Even without the existence of the state of Israel, the United States would probably still be distrusted and unwelcome because many throughout the Gulf and in the Third World perceive it as an imperialist power.

64. *FBIS*, 18 December 1981, p. C-3.

65. See Christopher Van Hollen, "Don't Engulf the Gulf," *Foreign Affairs* 59 (1980/81): 1064–78.

66. *FBIS*, 11 January 1982, p. C-1.

67. See Arnaud De Borchgrave, "Colossus of the Oil Lanes," *Newsweek*, 21 May 1973, p. 40.

7 | Conclusion: Gulf Security into the 1980s

John W. Amos, II, and Ralph H. Magnus

The preceding essays have focused attention on a number of issues bearing on Gulf security: the extent and impact of the Soviet invasion of Afghanistan, Iranian foreign and domestic policy, the regional dynamics of the Iraq-Iran war, the responses of local states to Gulf insecurities, and the quandaries of U.S. Middle Eastern policy. Now it is time to draw these threads together and to assess their meaning in terms of Gulf security for the next decade or so.

The first impression of Gulf security issues is that there are very few givens in the region that are not contested and controversial. On one such basic issue, nomenclature, we have decided to use the term "Gulf," rather than "Persian Gulf," as this area has been commonly designated in Western languages.[1] Whether the Gulf ought to be redesignated the "Arabian Gulf" or "Islamic Gulf" is, in our opinion, a modern political question beyond our purview. Difficulties over the area's name, however, aptly illustrate one of the basic sources of regional insecurity—the clash between Arab and Iranian ethnicities and their respective nationalist extensions.

Even the geographical dimensions of the Gulf region are subject to varying definitions. In large measure, controversies over the scope of security problems and their possible solutions are based on divergent geographical definitions of the Gulf.[2] Gulf security in its broadest sense may logically be seen to

The views, opinions, and/or findings contained in this report are those of the authors and should not be construed as an official Department of the Navy position, policy, or decision.

involve the entire world as the region becomes a major focus of superpower conflict. In concrete terms, the United States Rapid Deployment Joint Task Force (RDJTF; renamed the U.S. Central Command in January 1983) includes planning facilities in the Azores and Morocco, as well as troop units, squadrons, and vessels based in the continental United States. No doubt, a similar inventory of Soviet forces earmarked for the region would include units and bases from the Kola peninsula to Kamchatka.

The security of the Gulf can be seen as dependent on the entire strategic balance between the East and the West.[3] While perhaps a necessary concept for grand strategy, such a definition would be unwieldy for the dimensions of this study. Indeed, as one author has noted, such overly broad definitions of the problem can serve as a means of avoiding the real problems peculiar to the Gulf.[4] At the opposite end of the spectrum are definitions that, with equal logic, consider only the immediate vicinities of the major oil fields—or of the Saudi fields alone—as constituting a valid security concept of the Gulf.[5] In this view, it is there that the vital resources needing protection are located and not in every sand dune of the Rub al-Khali or mountain peak of the Elburz.

The contributors to this volume, which grew out of a panel presented at the Middle East Studies Association's annual meeting in 1981, through their individual treatment of their subject have arrived at a working definition of the Gulf practical enough for security problems. In this analysis, its definition includes the entire territories of the states bordering on the Gulf, as well as certain contiguous and neighboring areas vital to the security of the Gulf proper. The latter include Afghanistan, Pakistan, the Yemens, Turkey, the Horn of Africa, and the northwest quadrant of the Indian Ocean. Obviously, we have been unable to cover each of these areas here, but Afghanistan may be taken as representative of the importance of these peripheral areas to Gulf security. From a strictly military standpoint, some of them might be expendable in a campaign to defend the Gulf, as Joshua Epstein suggests may be the case with northern Iran.[6] However, we feel that our concept of security for the Gulf must include, at least, the political and psychological impact of military actions in such regions as northern Iran that might render defense of the oil areas impossible.

What, then, is our concept of "security" in relation to the Gulf? The first point is that Gulf security is a complex problem. Analytically it may be possible to distinguish between its various dimensions, but real security issues are invariably complex combinations, arranged in ever-shifting patterns, of the following elements:

1. Autonomous internal socio-economic change having implications for internal political stability;

2. Traditional territorial, tribal, and dynastic disputes and distrust hindering cooperation and possibly leading to conflicts;
3. Regional conflicts, both those involving Gulf states and those involving forces such as Israel, the Palestinians, or Libya;
4. Soviet aggression, either direct or through regional proxies and involving a broad spectrum from diplomatic threats to armed attack.

The Perceptual Dimension: Images and Realities of Superpower Threats

Any discussion of Gulf security must include the element of perception. Threats vary in the eye of the beholder; even when there is agreement on the elements involved in a threat, the weight to be given to each and the consequent mix of responses appropriate in each case remain highly controversial. In truth, there are as many interpretations of security as there are actors. For practical purposes, however, there is a broad distinction between the perceptions of the regional states and those of the United States. Although recognizing the importance of internal and regional threats, the Americans tend to stress the aspect of Soviet aggression. Similarly, the regional states might agree on the reality of some degree of Soviet threat, but naturally stress the localized challenges to their security. Neither position is correct or incorrect per se, nor is the problem capable of any hard-and-fast solution. What is needed, in our view, is mutual understanding and sensitivity on each side to the differing perceptions of the other.

Are these differences, however, merely perceptual, or are they reflections of fundamentally different interests? We must at least admit such a possibility. Because of its vast oil resources, the Gulf has become vital to the West. So vital, in fact, as to warrant the commitment of virtually the entire strategic conventional reserve of the United States to its defense. Clearly, the maintenance of Western access to this resource and, even more important, the prevention of Soviet control animate the Western commitment to Gulf security. Presumably, all Gulf states are equally interested in preventing Soviet intervention. Most of them have but recently gained their independence from foreign domination and even more recently secured control over their oil resources. They share in the Western perception that these resources are vital for the security and prosperity of the world as a whole. This shared interest is the underlying reality behind a common perception of a threat from the Soviets, however proximate or remote such a threat might be judged.

But this same basic premise—that the oil resources of the Gulf are vital to the Western industrialized nations—generates an alternative threat from the point of view of the Gulf states: the possibility that the West might want to seize control of these resources by military means. There is, admittedly, a certain logic behind this view. It repeats the very recent historical pattern of the British imperium. In addition, U.S. statements as recently as the Arab oil embargo of 1973–74 openly hinted at such action.[7] Finally, it is a theme reinforced regularly by Soviet propaganda.[8]

Although not impossible, a Western takeover is clearly a remote danger compared to the possibility of Soviet aggression. In the first place, Gulf oil is critical to the West. Any attempt to seize it by force would cause an intolerable period of economic disruption, even presuming that production could be revived over the opposition of the local populations. This is precisely what the West wants to avoid. More important, continued peaceful economic relationships involving the exchange of Gulf oil for Western goods, services, and technology are in the immediate and long-range interest of both sides. Finally, a Western attempt to seize Gulf oil would undoubtedly drive the regional states into the arms of the Soviet Union; this would be the worst possible outcome from the standpoint of the West.

Soviet aggression, however, is inherently much more plausible. It follows the historical tendencies of Russian and Soviet expansionism—tendencies confirmed in German-Soviet negotiations in 1940 and illustrated most recently by the acquisition of bases and clients in areas surrounding the Gulf and culminating in the invasion of Afghanistan. The Gulf region, even without oil, is an important geopolitical objective. In 1903, five years before the discovery of oil in Persia, the British foreign secretary, Lord Lansdowne, proclaimed that the waters of the Gulf were not open to any foreign naval base. By "any" he specifically meant Russian.[9] The land and sea route from the southern USSR to Gulf and Indian Ocean ports and thence to the Far Eastern regions of the USSR might be of crucial importance to the Soviets in the event of conflict with China.[10]

In contrast to those of the West, the vital interests of the Soviet Union do not at this time require Gulf oil. However, they might very well require it in the near future as the USSR's own energy reserves decline.[11] As the greatest continental (actually bicontinental) power in history, the Russian-Soviet empire consistently has emphasized self-sufficiency in vital natural resources. Unfortunately for Soviet strategists, there would seem to be no way short of armed force, or at least extreme coercion, to secure these resources for the Soviets in competition with the West. The Soviet economy is incapable of outbidding the West for the resources of the Gulf in any kind of a free and fair economic competition. Even military equipment, the resource for which the Soviets might find ready buyers, has been seriously devalued as a result of its performance in the Israeli invasion of Lebanon in 1982.

Barring a credible Western deterrent, a Soviet move to seize the oil of the Gulf is thus plausible. Indeed, the 1980s may well be the last decade in which four crucial elements are in the correct combination for Soviet strategists:

1. Current Gulf production is vital to the West, but not to the Soviets—meaning that a disruption could fatally tip the correlation of forces in favor of the Soviets;

2. Production could be restored, even after extensive disruption during combat operations or by deliberate destruction by retreating forces, in time for Gulf oil to be available to meet future Soviet needs;

3. The Gulf states are still suffering from the disruptions and distractions following the Iranian Islamic revolution, and the Gulf Cooperation Council (GCC) has yet to establish itself as a major security factor;

4. The Western deterrent, in the form of the RDJTF, is still too underdeveloped to form a credible conventional deterrent.

In these circumstances, Soviet military action almost becomes a "no lose" situation. If the Soviets win, they deny the resources to the West and have time to rebuild them for their own future needs. But if they are unable to seize the oil fields for themselves, the destruction wrought to the production and transportation facilities might well damage them enough to deny the oil resources to the West for a considerable period of time. Although it might be argued that such an attack would unify the Western alliance in the short run, in the long run it might increase Western European dependence on Soviet energy supplies. Arguably, the same conditions apply to the nature of the deterrent and its credibility in the Gulf as in other regions. Even though the oil of the Gulf is vital and the United States has declared in unmistakable terms that it will use military force for its protection, a purely declaratory deterrent dependent on a general nuclear war for its credibility is, in fact, not credible when confronted with a serious conventional capability on the part of the enemy. It must be assumed after Afghanistan that the Soviet Union has such a capability in this region.[12]

Perceptions of threats stemming from the first three components of Gulf security—internal, traditional, and regional conflicts—are not as divergent as sometimes alleged. Both the regional states and the West regard these threats as being, in practice, the most likely.[13] The inherent clash of Western security policies and those of the Gulf states arise because necessary preparations to counter the Soviet threat, which can be undertaken by the United States only with a certain minimal amount of local cooperation, are seen by some states as weakening their internal security and exposing them to regional threats—particularly from Iran.[14] Here again, we may trace some underlying differences of interests behind the differences in perceptions. And again, this difference arises because the Western commitment is predominantly linked to an interest in Gulf oil. There is a logic, confirmed by recent historical examples, that argues that the flow of Gulf oil is not dependent on the existence of any particular type of political regime in the Gulf (except, of course, a communist regime). Iraq in 1958 and Iran two decades later both changed their regimes drastically, yet economic imperatives led each to continue the pre-existing practice of exchanging oil for Western goods and services. This occurred despite the Arab nationalist, anti-imperialist ideology of the Iraqi revolution and the even more extreme rhetoric of the Iranian revolution, which specifically aimed at ending Iran's economic dependence on oil exports. Given this historical record and the continuing heavy dependence of all Gulf economies on oil exports, it might be argued that although the existing regimes have a clear interest in their own survival, the West might well be able to live with a variety of regimes since all of them will need to export oil to their natural markets in the West. Indeed, from a purely cynical point of view of Western interests, it might be advantageous to have a high degree of tension, division, and insecurity in the Gulf as a means of weakening the effective bargaining power of OPEC and the Organization of Arab Petroleum Exporting Countries.[15]

Fortunately, Western policymakers reject this viewpoint. It is a false distinction. Its flaw lies in the complexity of Gulf security issues, which dictate indivisible connections among the various threats. Any diminution of Gulf security, from whatever quarter, eventually reflects on the ability of the Gulf states to defend themselves against other threats, including the worst-case (from the Western point of view) threat of the Soviet Union.

Internal Threats and Traditional Disputes

From the perspective of Gulf leaders, their most immediate security problems stem from stresses inherent in a situation of unbelievably rapid socioeconomic change in the context of political structures still in their formative stage. Until only a decade or two past, the region had been largely bypassed by the currents of development, nationalism, and political change taking place elsewhere in the Middle East. The processes of the creation of new social classes, the establishment of fixed frontiers, new political institutions, and, above all, the creation of a modern economy based on petroleum all have had the potential of creating new security threats. Even a brief glance at recent history clearly reveals that some of these threats already have been realized.

Bahrain and Kuwait, for example, each had their very national existence challenged by their large neighbors at the time they gained independence. These neighbors, Iran and Iraq, both claimed that Bahrain and Kuwait were lost provinces separated from their respective fatherlands by British imperialism. The very concept of fixed international boundaries was (and still is) new to the Gulf: "The concept of territorial sovereignty in the Western sense did not exist in Eastern Arabia," wrote J. B. Kelly in the 1960s.[16] In 1981 John

Duke Anthony could list no less than eight outstanding territorial disputes in the Gulf as "more important" and usually involving an outside power supporting one or the other side.[17] In the midst of the crisis situations created by the Iran-Iraq war and the attempted coup in Bahrain, the ministerial meeting of the GCC in March 1982 was forced to devote most of its efforts to restoring the status quo in a territorial dispute between two of its members, Bahrain and Qatar, over the Hawar Islands. The source of the dispute lay in Qatar's angry reaction to Bahrain's naming a naval unit the "Hawar" and holding military maneuvers in the disputed area.[18] Deep-rooted familial and tribal hatreds occur not only between states but within states and ruling families. In some cases, intra-elite conflicts have led to palace coups and political assassinations.

In addition, most (if not all) of the states of the Gulf are characterized by the presence of traditional political and social structures—structures that are by and large patriarchal in nature. However, the forces generated by recent oil-related wealth, and the concomitant processes of social change (especially urbanization), have created a broader educated and politically knowledgeable public. Many of these occupy crucial positions in the state bureaucracy and in the largely laissez-faire economic system. Thus, the domestic environment of policy formation is bifurcated between patriarchal elite and the increasingly politicized masses. When the powerful but incalculable influence emanating from the Iranian Islamic revolution is added, the ruling elites are faced with a politically delicate situation.

Efforts to modify traditional political structures to give constitutional participation and representation to new social classes, such as the intellectuals and industrial workers, have been made in a number of Gulf states. Although strictly limited in scope and power, the elected assemblies in both Kuwait and Bahrain had to be suspended by the rulers (the Kuwaiti assembly, however, was revived following the elections of 23 February 1981).

Underlying the security situation in all but a few Gulf countries is the demographic fact of large populations of foreigners, in many cases amounting to actual majorities, possessing not even the traditional tribal political right of appeal to the ruler in his *majlis*. In an unguarded moment, Abdullah Bishara, the secretary general of the GCC, even went so far as to admit that this was a greater problem for Gulf security than was the Israeli threat: "Frankly, before I confront the Israelis on the Golan, I, as a Gulf citizen, should face a problem that is threatening me and that will make me a victim: the problem of foreign immigration to the region."[19] It is thus hardly surprising that the Gulf states first want to put their own house in order before taking on such weighty issues as the Soviet-U.S. rivalry in their region.

Polarization in the Middle East:
Regional Conflicts with Global Implications

The war in Lebanon, which dramatically escalated with the Israeli invasion of July 1982, clearly altered the political and military balance in the Levant. It may also, however, have set in motion trends in Middle Eastern politics as a whole whose ultimate impact is as yet unforeseeable. Nevertheless, dramatic as the events in Lebanon are, they are still connected to the other war, the Iraq-Iran war. It is the connection, the linkage between the two conflicts, that will define the nature of regional threats to Gulf security for some time to come. Indeed, the connection between the two wars was never more obvious than in the timing of the Israeli attack on Lebanon and that of the subsequent Iranian invasion of Iraq. For their part, the Israelis appear to have counted on the fact that Syria's support for Iranian war efforts had effectively isolated it from the majority of the Arab world. Conversely, the Iranians were clearly aware that Arab disarray over Lebanon (and in fact world concern over the possibility that the war there might spread) would leave them essentially free to do as they wished against Iraq.

This linkage, either perceptual (in the minds of Arab decision makers) or actual (in terms of concrete political and military relations), compounds the problems of assuring Gulf security. However, the linkage phenomenon extends both spatially and sociologically throughout the area. The net result is that security problems and threats tend to have a multiplicity of dimensions and sources. Along these lines, there are a number of possible regional threats to Gulf security.

To the west, the aggressive forward policy currently pursued by the Libyans constitutes a potential, if distant, threat. At present, Libyan policy seems focused on creating a Central African Islamic state under its own auspices. However, the Aden Treaty Alliance of Libya, South Yemen, and Ethiopia may prove to be the vehicle for extending Libya's influence much farther east, into the Gulf itself.

To the north, the outcome of the Iraq-Iran war will determine the nature of the threat. If the Iranians win, Iranian-sponsored Islamic fundamentalism, backed by Iranian military force, will become the dominant security concern. If the Iraqis win, Iraqi-sponsored pan-Arabism backed by Iraqi forces may well become the major destabilizing influence. Alternatively, if the governments of one or both of the combatants collapse under the pressure of continued fighting, the ensuing anarchy could spread southward.

But if the war develops into a prolonged stalemate (and this is a likely prospect since neither side has the logistic capabilities necessary to drive on the other's capital),[20] the continued stability of Iran itself, simply due to the prospects of a conflict over succession to Khomeini, will become an increasingly important factor in Gulf security. It would seem logical to expect militant Iranian political organizations to engage in increasingly aggressive maneuvering in order to be in a position to attempt (or prevent) a coup. The temptation to pre-empt will increase with each year, as Khomeini grows older. An ensuing civil war in Iran would have repercussions throughout the Gulf, with or without any Soviet intervention. However, the Soviets could well be expected to abandon their heretofore cautious movement into Iran in favor of direct military force—if for no other reason than to stabilize their own borders.[21]

Spillover from Arab-Israeli tensions to the west may yet directly affect the Gulf. This could result from a projection of Israeli power, either down the Red Sea or overland toward Syria and Iraq, in response to any number of combinations of Rejection Front/Palestinian military activities stemming from the invasion of Lebanon. Alternatively, it could result from organizational activities of major Palestinian groups displaced from Lebanon—groups that could seek to turn one or more Gulf states into a substitute base of operations. Also, splinter groups with little or no connection to mainline Palestinian organizations could attempt to destabilize the Gulf. Although the Gulf states are in the process of developing their security forces, these forces are still relatively weak. The lack of an effectively organized network of security forces combined with a concentration of vulnerable oil-producing facilities makes the Gulf a logical target of opportunity for Palestinian extremists.

The Architechtonics of U.S. Policy: Strategy and Security in the Gulf

As MacDonald so ably points out, the initial U.S. policy response to Soviet Afghan moves was to create a deterrent force, the Rapid Deployment Force (RDF; later reconstituted as the RDJTF), to counter Soviet military moves. The original idea here was to signal the Soviet Union that any further movement toward the Gulf, and in particular toward Gulf oil fields, would trigger a U.S. military response of unknown dimensions. The RDF itself was to be both the symbol of the U.S. determination and a physical tripwire to block any direct Soviet military moves.[22]

Originally, the RDF was envisioned as a strictly military response to an external threat to Gulf oil-producing regions. Much of the literature dealing with this aspect of the RDJTF revolves around the issue of whether it is indeed a credible military force. However, another body of literature raises a different issue: namely, whether the RDJTF can be effective at all given the premise

5. Waltz, "Rapid Deployment Force."

6. Epstein, "Soviet Vulnerabilities," pp. 130–37.

7. The best known of these warnings of military action was undoubtedly the interview with Secretary of State Henry Kissinger ("Kissinger on Oil, Food and Trade," *Business Week*, 13 January 1975, pp. 66-76). Its text was distributed in the Middle East by the U.S. Information Service and was reproduced in the authoritative *Middle East Economic Survey* 18, no. 12 (10 January 1975). In fact, the entire tenor of the interview was on political and economic actions and not hostile to the interests of the oil producers. The reply to the question on the use of military force, by its reference to the Vietnam war in calling it a "very dangerous course," to be resorted to only in the case of "actual strangulation of the industrialized world" was itself very much against the use of military force.

For other well-publicized discussions on U.S. seizure of Arab oil fields, see Robert W. Tucker, "Oil: The Issue of American Interventions," *Commentary*, January 1975, pp. 21-31; Miles Ignotus, "Seizing Arab Oil," *Harper's*, March 1975, pp. 45-62; U.S. Congress, House, Committee on International Relations, *Oil Fields as Military Objectives: A Feasibility Study* (Washington, D.C.: Government Printing Office, 1975); and Edward Friedland, Paul Seabury, and Aaron Wedovsky, *The Great Détente Disaster, Oil, and the Decline of American Foreign Policy* (New York: Basic Books, 1975).

8. The Kissinger interview in *Business Week* was immediately picked up by *Pravda*; see Leonid Medvedko, "Who Is Pushing an Oil War?" *Pravda*, 7 January 1975; reproduced in *Current Digest of the Soviet Press* 27, no. 1 (29 January 1975): 17. See also Lenczowski, "An Encircling Strategy," pp. 312–13.

9. Lenczowski, "An Encircling Strategy," p. 319.

10. Lt. Cdr. James T. Westwood, "The Relentless March," *Army*, June 1969, p. 66. Westwood was director of the Combat Capabilities Analysis Group of the RDJTF.

11. There is certainly no unanimity of Western views on Soviet oil production. If anything, the most widely held view is that the Soviets have ample energy, but serious problems with its location and distribution (see Arthur Jay Klinghoffer, *The Soviet Union and International Oil Politics* [New York: Columbia University Press, 1977], pp. 38-57; and Leslie Dienes, "Energy Self-Sufficiency in the Soviet Union," *Current History* 69, no. 407 [July/August 1975]: 10-14., 47-51). On the other hand, the controversial reports of the CIA issued publicly in April and July 1977, *Prospects for Soviet Oil Production* and *Prospects for Soviet Oil: Supplementary Analysis*, cannot be entirely dismissed.

12. Evidently this is the assumption that was made at the time by U.S. defense leaders. See the statement by General David C. Jones, chairman of the Joint Chiefs of Staff, on "Good Morning America," 30 January 1980: "The Soviet invasion of Afghanistan changed the equation in the world very, very significantly. The Soviets since World War II have not used their military forces outside their own territory or in Eastern Europe and the Warsaw Pact area. So it indicated a step in escalation. I'm not predicting World War III. But I don't believe the Soviet objective in the Middle East is

that the major source of threat to Gulf security is internal, from dome discontent, rather than Soviet penetration. The argument is that the RD may be counterproductive because a U.S. presence might serve as a lightı rod to spark antigovernment activities.[23] Yet a third point of view suggests Gulf politics is so closely intertwined with Arab-Israeli issues that any U policy attempting to isolate Gulf security measures from a solution to Palestinian question is doomed to failure. As Anthony points out, the C states' perceptions of threats to their security are heavily influenced by a se that it is the Israelis, rather than the Soviets, who are the real threat.

Whatever the truth of any of these views, taken together they illustrate problem of policy formation vis-à-vis areas as complex as the Middle Eas general and the Gulf in particular. The Middle East is one of the most diffi‹ of all foreign policy environments. As an area of policy concern, the Mid East presents a combination of great uncertainty and great necessity—unc‹ tainty because the prevailing pattern of conflicts is both complicated ‹ volatile; necessity because of the Middle East's central geographical locat and because it is the repository of a very high percentage of world oil reserv

Notes

1. For an exhaustive and authoritative discussion of this issue, see C. Edmu Bosworth, "The Nomenclature of the Persian Gulf," in Alvin J. Cottrell, ed., 7 *Persian Gulf States* (Baltimore, Md.: Johns Hopkins University Press, 1980), ‹ xvii–xxxiv.

2. Some of the major contributions to this subject are Hossein Amirsadeghi, e‹ *The Security of the Persian Gulf* (London: Croom Helm, 1981); Shahram Chubi "Soviet Policy Toward Iran and the Gulf," *Adelphi Papers*, no. 157 (1980); James ‹ Noyes, *The Clouded Lens: Persian Gulf Security and U.S. Policy*, 2d ed. (Stanfor Hoover Institution Press, 1982); Jeffrey Record, *The Rapid Deployment Force and l Military Intervention in the Persian Gulf* (Cambridge, Mass., and Washington, D.C Institute for Foreign Policy Analysis, 1981); Joshua M. Epstein, "Soviet Vu nerabilities in Iran and the RDF Deterrent," *International Security* 6, no. 2 (F‹ 1981): 126–58; Hermann F. Eilts, "Security Considerations in the Persian Gulf *International Security* 5, no. 2 (Fall 1980): 79–112; George Lenczowski, "The Sovi‹ Union and the Persian Gulf: An Encircling Strategy," *International Journal* 37, no. (1982): 307–27; Dennis Ross, "Considering Soviet Threats to the Persian Gulf *International Security* 6, no. 2 (Fall 1981): 159–80; W. Scott Thompson, "The Persia Gulf and the Correlation of Forces," *International Security* 7, no. 1 (Summer 1982 157–80; Kenneth N. Waltz, "A Strategy for the Rapid Deployment Force," *Interna tional Security* 5, no. 4 (Spring 1981): 49–73; and David D. Newsom, "Americ Engulfed," *Foreign Policy* 43 (Summer 1981): 17–32.

3. Thompson, "Correlation of Forces," adopts such an approach.

4. Epstein, "Soviet Vulnerabilities," especially pp. 127–28 and 157–58.

Afghanistan. They have an expansionist policy." (Quoted in Ralph H. Magnus, "The Carter Doctrine: New Directions on a Familiar Stage," *Journal of the American Institute for the Study of Middle Eastern Civilization* 1, no. 2 [Summer 1980]: 7.)

13. The agreement on this issue is sometimes disputed and indeed, there may have been some shift in the United States' views; see the article by George C. Wilson, "US Plans Maneuvers with Oman," *Washington Post*, 25 August 1982, p. 1, in which he notes: "As a result of the Reagan administration's review of its Persian Gulf policy, the Pentagon has put top priority on finding ways to protect such friendly Arab governments from being toppled by radicals. Direct military assaults against Persian Gulf fields are regarded only as a secondary threat in the Pentagon's revised war plans."

14. Iranian leaders constantly warn the Arabs of the dangers of association with the United States for their security, linking the conservative Arab governments to Israel through the United States. In a November 1981 Friday sermon, Hojjatul-Islam Hashemi-Rafsanjani used the proposed "Fahd Peace Plan" as a case in point: "The US Bright Star maneuvers were held only to give support and assurance to the gentlemen who are going to gather in Fes to vote for the plan. The US is trying to tell these gentlemen not to be afraid, the US is here, the US is with you; US paratroopers and marines can land rapidly; do not be afraid of the people who can come quickly." (See "Fahd Peace Plan Scored in 20 November Demonstrations," *Foreign Broadcast Information Service* (FBIS) *South Asia*, 23 November 1981, p. I-6, reporting a Tehran domestic service broadcast in Persian of 20 November 1981.)

15. The regional states are well aware of their lessened bargaining power due to the decline of their oil production and their market shares in a situation of oversupply, resulting in cutthroat competition among Gulf producers (see 'Abd al-Karim al-Khalif, "So That We Are Not Drowned in Oil," *al-Yamamah* [Riyadh] 668 [12/18 February 1982]; *Joint Publications Research Service [JPRS]* 2524 [13 April 1982]: 125–29).

16. J. B. Kelly, *Eastern Arabian Frontiers* (New York: Praeger, 1964), p. 18. See also R. Michael Burrell and Keith McLachlan, "The Political Geography of the Persian Gulf," in Cottrell, *The Persian Gulf States,* pp. 121–28.

17. John Duke Anthony, "The Persian Gulf in Regional and International Politics: The Arab Side of the Gulf," in Amirsadeghi, *Security*, pp. 171–72.

18. Sulayman Nimr, "After the Qatar-Bahrain Dispute Flared Up, Gulf Solidarity Met Its First Test," *al-Mustaqbal* (Paris) 264 (13 March 1982): 32; trans. as "Efforts to End Qatar-Bahrain Dispute Discussed," *JPRS* 80462 (2 June 1982): 7–9.

19. "Daily Quotes Bisharah Remarks on Gulf Problems," *FBIS*, 20 January 1982, p. C-2, quoting a report in *al-Shariqah al-Khalij* (Manama), 16 January 1982, p. 1.

20. The Iranians, for example, have an enormous edge in manpower, but have so far been unable to follow up or consolidate any gains due to this edge. The Iraqis have sufficient forces to defend Iraqi territory, but not enough to drive the Iranians back into the interior of Iran.

21. Alvin Z. Rubinstein, "The Soviet Union and Iran under Khomeini," *International Affairs* 57 (1981): 599–617.

22. Magnus, "Carter Doctrine"; Record, *Rapid Deployment Force*; and Joe Stork, "The Carter Doctrine and US Bases in the Middle East," *MERIP Reports*, no. 90 (September 1980): 3–14.

23. See the literature already cited and Christopher van Hollen, "Don't Engulf the Gulf," *Foreign Affairs* 59 (1980/81): 1064–78; Valerie York, "Security in the Gulf: A Strategy of Preemption," *The World Today* 36 (July 1980): 239–50; and John C. Campbell, "Soviet Policy in the Middle East," *Current History* 80 (January 1981): 1–4, 42–43.

Contributors

JOHN W. AMOS, II, teaches Middle Eastern Politics at the Naval Postgraduate School, Monterey, California. He holds a Ph.D. in Political Science from the University of California at Berkeley and a J.D. from the Monterey College of Law. He has written two books, *Arab-Israeli Military/Political Relations* and the *Palestinian Resistance*, and a number of articles on Middle Eastern politics.

JOHN DUKE ANTHONY is President of the National Council on U.S.-Arab Relations in Washington, D.C., and a Fellow of the Johns Hopkins Foreign Policy Institute. He was an Associate Professor of Middle East Studies at the Johns Hopkins School of Advanced International Studies (SAIS) in Washington, D.C., and has also been a Visiting Professor at the Woodrow Wilson School of Foreign Affairs of the University of Virginia, at the Center for Middle East Studies of the University of Texas, and at the Wharton School of Finance and Commerce of the University of Pennsylvania in Philadelphia. Dr. Anthony holds graduate degrees from the School of Foreign Service of Georgetown University and SAIS. He has published several books and has coauthored numerous books on the Middle East.

ROBERT G. DARIUS (Irani) joined the Historical Office in the U.S. Army Materiel Development and Readiness Command Headquarters in Alexandria, Virginia, as the Senior Logistics Historian in mid-June 1983. He was a member of the Faculty of the Strategic Studies Institute, the U.S. Army's in-house "think tank," U.S. Army War College, Carlisle Barracks, Pennsylvania, 1975–1983. He has an M.A. from the School of International Service, American University, Washington, D.C., and another M.A. and a Ph.D. in government and politics and international relations from the University of Maryland, College Park. Dr. Darius's professional background includes extensive travels on both sides of the Gulf area and one year of field research at the Institute for International Political and Economic Studies, Tehran. He has written many articles and monographs in Farsi and English for professional journals.

GEORGE LENCZOWSKI, Professor of Political Science at the University of California, Berkeley, is a Senior Research Fellow of the Hoover Institution and adviser to the Middle Eastern studies program. His books on the region include *The Middle East and World Affairs* (4th ed.), *Iran under the Pahlavis*, and *Middle East Oil in a Revolutionary Age*.

CHARLES G. MACDONALD, Associate Professor of International Relations at Florida International University, is author of *Iran, Saudi Arabia, and the Law of the Sea* (1980) and co-editor of *Revolution in Iran: A Reappraisal* (1983). He earned an M.A. and a Ph.D. in Foreign Affairs at the University of Virginia. He is currently writing a monograph on the Kurdish question in Islamic Iran.

RALPH H. MAGNUS is Associate Professor and Coordinator of Middle East Studies at the Naval Postgraduate School, Monterey, California. He was educated at the University of California, Berkeley, where he earned his doctorate in 1971. In 1971–72 he was a postdoctoral Peace Fellow at the Hoover Institution. He has published a number of articles and contributed chapters on Middle East international relations, oil, the Persian Gulf, and Afghanistan and is the editor of *Documents on the Middle East* (Washington, D.C.: American Enterprise Institute, 1969). He served as Assistant Cultural Attaché of the American embassy in Kabul (1963–1965) and is currently the Executive Director of Americares for Afghans, a foundation providing medical aid to Afghan refugees.

Index

HOOVER INTERNATIONAL STUDIES